Responding to

Adolescents

Helping relationship skills for youth workers, mentors and other advisors

Angela M. Taylor

RHP

Russell House Publishing

First published in 2003 by:
Russell House Publishing Ltd.
4 St. George's House
Uplyme Road
Lyme Regis
Dorset DT7 3LS

Tel: 01297–443948
Fax: 01297–442722
e-mail: help@russellhouse.co.uk
www.russellhouse.co.uk

British Library Cataloguing-in-publication Data:
A catalogue record for this book is available from the British Library.

ISBN: 1-903855-28-4
Typeset by Saxon Graphics Ltd, Derby
Cover design by Lee Simmons
Printed by Antony Rowe, Chippenham

About Russell House Publishing

- RHP is a group of social work, probation, education and youth and community work practitioners and academics working in collaboration with a professional publishing team.
- Our aim is to work closely with the field to produce innovative and valuable materials to help managers, trainers, practitioners and students.
- We are keen to receive feedback on publications and new ideas for future projects.
- For details of our other publications please visit our website or ask us for a catalogue. Contact details are on this page.

Contents

Preface   iv
Acknowledgements   iv

Introduction   1

Section One: Relationship Skills   5
  1. The Value and Aims of a Helping Relationship   5
  2. Responsible Working Practice   12
  3. Interpersonal Skills: 25
    Key Qualities, Prejudices and Communication Skills
  4. Beginnings   33

Section Two: Adolescents' Relationships   39
  5. Parents   39
  6. Changing Family Relationships: Separation, Divorce and   47
    Re-marriage
  7. Cultural Identities   52
  8. Peer Relationships: Positive Development and Negative   60
    Influences

Section Three: Recognising and Responding to Concerns   67
  9. Bullying   67
 10. Drugs and Alcohol: Users and Abusers   72
 11. In Trouble: Criminal Offending   81
 12. Sexuality and Sexual Relationships   92
 13. Teenage Pregnancy, Teenage Mothers and Teenage Fathers   106
 14. Overwhelming Emotions: Stress, Depression,   116
    Suicidal Thoughts, Self-injury and Eating Disorders
 15. Death, Bereavement and Other Loss   130
 16. Leaving Home   138

Section Four: Referring and Ending   145
 17. Referrals and Endings   145
 18. A Final Word   152

References   154

Preface

The inspiration for this book has come from my enjoyment of work and research with adolescents over many years. My professional work as a Chartered Psychologist, counsellor and lecturer together with my complementary roles as youth court magistrate and voluntary youth worker have enabled me to meet young people from diverse backgrounds. They have allowed me to get to know them, work with them and gain insight into different aspects of their lives. This has been a great privilege.

Research from the fields of psychology and counselling provide the underpinning knowledge base of the book. Where a source is not given, the guidance and practical suggestions have been drawn from my experience amalgamated with generally accepted counselling practice. The case study examples have been drawn from my own interactions with young people. These are essentially genuine although some are 'composites' and names and details have been changed to ensure that individuals cannot be identified. My thanks are due to the young people from whom I have learnt and am still learning.

Angela Taylor PhD
April 2003

Acknowledgements

Many people have helped me, both directly and indirectly, in the production of this book. Firstly I thank Jenny Nemko for suggesting that I write, for her clear advice in the early stages, and for her sustaining enthusiasm which has made this an enjoyable project. I must also thank all my peer reviewers for their constructive criticism and encouragement. They include Viola Nzira, lecturer in Youth and Community Studies at the University of Reading, counsellors Cynthia Zneimer, Elizabeth Edwards and Barbara Jackson, International Student Adviser Shahnaz Raven and Youth Offending Team Manager Richard Segalov and his colleagues. Particular thanks go to my colleague Dr Judy Turner for her patient understanding about my preoccupation with this book and for commenting on various drafts. As ever my clinical supervisor Cassie Cooper has been a tower of strength. In the final stages Geoffrey Mann and Martin Jones of Russell House Publishing have been extremely supportive and I have enjoyed working with Lee Simmons who designed the book cover. Finally, but foremost, thanks to my husband David for his unstinting support and love.

Introduction

How to respond?

Disheartened, Julie watched 14 year old Lisa leave for home earlier than planned. Julie knew that she had let Lisa down.

Lisa had been attending a week's residential drama workshop, run by voluntary youth workers for under-achieving inner city teenagers. Julie, an artist, was organising the painting of the stage backdrops for the drama production at the end of the week. In addition she had been asked to look after a group of six girls. She had thought she could manage that...but she hadn't been prepared for Lisa.

Lisa had been painting haphazardly and looking fed up. Only the day before they had been chatting happily while working together, so Julie asked if she was feeling okay. Lisa replied that she was wishing that she hadn't come away. Then Julie found herself promising to keep a secret as Lisa talked about her mother.

With Lisa away her mother's 'repulsive' new boyfriend might take the chance to stay over at their flat and she was worried about her mother. 'Dunno what she sees in him. Anyway Mum isn't answering her phone and I can't get through to her...and what's more...this week away is rubbish.' (Julie was beginning to feel uncomfortable.) 'Anyway the girls in my room are always having a go at me...' (Julie busied herself with the painting so she could sort of listen without being too involved.) '...if only they'd leave me alone...'

Julie suddenly felt back in her depth – she should and could do something! 'Oh I could talk to them.'

Lisa snapped 'Who said you should interfere? You said you wouldn't talk to anyone. You'll just make it worse. Just like the rest...you haven't a clue!' Julie tried to retrieve the situation but Lisa stormed off. Not sure of what to do, Julie felt duty-bound to keep the confidence.

Within the hour Lisa had found someone who was driving back to town...and she grabbed a lift. Julie had not expected that. Lisa had enjoyed the first couple of days and now Julie had blown all the good it had done, just by saying the wrong thing. If only she had known how to respond.

Troubled adolescents are unlikely to seek help directly. Some, like Lisa, may not believe that anyone else could possibly help but they may still confide in an older person whom they know. If Julie had stayed calm and listened attentively, with confidence in her own ability to be supportive, things may have turned out differently.

Why do adolescents need support?

Having to adapt to major changes and to face new challenges is stressful for most adults. Therefore it is not surprising that young people having to cope with a succession of significant changes and difficult challenges during adolescence find it a trying, confusing and stressful time. Adolescence is the term used for the period of transition from childhood to adulthood affecting all areas of life: physical, social, emotional, cognitive and educational development. Geldard and Geldard (1999) summarise the challenges of adolescence as including the following:

- Adjusting to physical changes in height, body shape and strength.
- Adjusting to sexual changes and developing sexual identity.
- Making new peer relationships – both same-sex and opposite-sex.
- Being able to manage emotional changes, mood swings and strong emotional feelings.
- Achieving independence from parents, emotionally and socially.
- Developing knowledge and skills to prepare for higher education, a job or a career and for (eventually) achieving economic independence.
- Developing socially responsible patterns of behaviour.
- Developing own system of values, attitudes and beliefs.

This is a lengthy process. It is also an erratic process with individuals maturing in some aspects of their life more quickly than others and then regressing when they hit a time of turbulence. Every adolescent faces some difficult times, although most will negotiate these by using their own strengths and the support of immediate family and friends. However, some adolescents do need additional help. Coleman and Hendry (1999) describe conditions which make periods of transition particularly difficult, as follows:

- When the 'bad' timing of a significant change creates additional stress, for example: early puberty.
- When outside events (leaving school, death of someone close) and internal changes (mood swings, loss after breaking up with first proper girl/boyfriend) occur simultaneously or cumulatively, so that the individual has to deal with too many things at once.
- When mental health issues arise (depression, eating disorders).
- When the young person's life context and their inner expectations lack 'goodness of fit', as for example, a poor school environment may disappoint or frustrate an academic adolescent; or having to move to a step-parent's home.

Adapted from Coleman and Hendry, 1999: p10.

Facing these sorts of difficulties, many adolescents, and especially those without supportive families, may well benefit from additional outside support.

Aim of this book

This book is written for youth workers, mentors, sports coaches, personal advisers, scout or guide leaders, project organisers, social workers, education welfare officers, school personal tutors, YOT workers, youth work students and others who work with adolescents. Based on knowledge and experience gained from practice and research in the fields of psychology and counselling, this book provides guidance for those working regularly or occasionally with young people aged between twelve and nineteen years. It suggests ways of giving support by combining interpersonal skills and basic counselling skills with practical advice. It provides information about the relationships and the problem areas which are of most concern to adolescents (Irwin, 2002) and suggests ways of responding both to crises and to ongoing difficulties. Some particularly sensitive and entrenched problem areas are indicated, where the young person should always be referred to qualified professionals for support. Above all the book suggests how to initiate, develop and end one-to-one relationships and so provide effective support.

The objectives of this book are to:

- Describe interpersonal skills and basic counselling skills which may encourage the adolescent to communicate.
- Suggest the professional safeguards needed for ethical practice, for the protection of both the adolescent and the youth worker.
- Describe relationships which are important to adolescents and may cause concern.
- Put problem areas into context, based on up-to-date research.
- Prepare the youth worker to contain anxiety at the time of crisis.
- Alert the youth worker to common pitfalls.
- Provide information for appropriate referral.
- Suggest methods of referral.

Content and format of the book

The book is divided into four parts. Part One introduces the idea of the helping relationship and describes the different skills that can be used to engage a young person and encourage communication. The basic helping skills are adapted from person-centred counselling models (Thorne, 1990; Nelson-Jones, 1997) but they are common to most other counselling approaches. Chapter 1 discusses the value of the one-to-one relationship and the realistic aims of a first helping relationship. Chapter 2 explains the supervision support for the youthworker to work safely and effectively. It describes some ethical issues to be considered and then suggests some working practice measures to protect the interests of both the young person and the youth worker. Chapter 3 discusses the positive personal qualities brought by the youth worker and then considers ways of recognising personal prejudices. Verbal and non-verbal communications skills are then introduced. Chapter 4 covers the practical issues to be addressed at the beginning of a relationship and suggests ways for encouraging communication.

Managing relationships is one of the hardest things about being a teenager (Irwin, 2002). To investigate this source of difficulty Part Two looks at the most significant relationships in the lives of adolescents. Chapter 5 discusses the positive and negative aspects of adolescents' relationships with their parents and suggests how positive relationships can be encouraged. Chapter 6 examines the difficulties that are faced when parents separate, divorce and find new partners. Chapter 7 looks at the identity development of young people from minority cultures and the difficulties when family or community values clash with those of the majority culture. Chapter 8 examines peer relationships, looking at how adolescents join peer groups and how they may be positively or negatively influenced.

Part Three explores eight major areas that are of most concern to adolescents (Irwin, 2002). Although these are presented separately for clarity, individuals frequently experience several overlapping areas of difficulty at the same time. Chapter 9 concentrates on bullying while Chapter 10 focuses on drug and alcohol abuse. Chapter 11 describes the factors which combine to increase the risk of adolescents breaking the law. It looks at ways of supporting those at risk of offending and co-operating with other agencies to maintain behavioural change. Chapter 12 examines adolescent concerns with issues of sexuality, including gay identity, and sexual relationships. Chapter 13 raises issues around teenage pregnancy and includes short sections on supporting teenage parents. Chapter 14 focuses on mental health issues including stress, depression, despair, self-injury, suicidal thinking and eating disorders. Ways to recognise and respond to each of them are suggested. Chapter 15 discusses how adolescents can be supported after the death of someone close to them. Chapter 16 looks at the issues involved in leaving home and the type of support that may be needed. These eight areas have been selected as central to this book, rather than concerns about education, jobs, careers and money. While young people may seek help openly with the latter, they tend to be reluctant to tackle the former due to embarrassment, guilt, shame or distress, even though the problems arising may disrupt their lives and their progress in education and employment. The Chief Executive of Connexions, the government backed youth work initiative, reported: 'Connexions is increasingly finding that personal development advice is as crucial as guidance about careers and education' (Weinstock, 2003: p11). The issues covered here are frequently difficult to recognise and acknowledge.

As the ending of a helpful relationship often has significant implications and should be sensitively managed, Part Four focuses on endings. Chapter 17 covers the practical and emotional aspects of preparing for endings, including referrals, planned endings and unexpected endings, while Chapter 18 summarises and concludes.

Throughout the book the terms 'youth worker', 'mentor' and 'helper' are used interchangeably to include everyone with an interest in supporting young people.

Realistic expectations

An individual youth worker cannot gain the expertise to deal with the whole range of difficulties which adolescents will face. Nevertheless they can help every individual adolescent by:

- Providing the experience of a positive relationship in which the adolescent feels respected and maintains their independence.
- Being a positive role model.
- Demonstrating that however dreadful a problem may appear, the youth worker will not be overwhelmed.
- Encouraging feelings of self-worth.
- Providing information and making appropriate referrals where necessary.

The value of even a short one-to-one relationship should not be underestimated.

SECTION ONE: RELATIONSHIP SKILLS

Chapter 1

The Value and Aims of a Helping Relationship

This chapter examines the purpose of the helping relationship and suggests some realistic aims. Relationships develop slowly, requiring patience and commitment. Although longer term mentoring relationships may not provide immediate signs of progress, such a relationship may enhance the personal development of the young person. Helping relationships may also act as stepping-stones for accessing other support.

No-one understands what I am going through…

My mother said that I'd grow out of it, but I'm still as…

I know I've got to do it, but I can't face it…

I've never told anyone before but…

My old class teacher tried to help but then she left the school…

While one young person may need specialist help to confront their difficulties, another may need only some friendly support to get through a particularly trying period. Often the individual is within reach of the help that is needed but unable to access it. For some adolescents past experiences with unreliable or unresponsive adults have made them wary about asking for help. Some cannot find the right words while others do not have the confidence to ask. Some do not recognise that they have reached the stage of a problem where only outside intervention can help. Others feel unworthy of taking anyone else's time. Some feel that their problems may be so unusual or so 'bad, sad or mad' that no-one will be able to help.

Preparing to support adolescents involves recognising when there is the need for help and developing the skills to respond in a way that will be appropriate, acceptable and helpful.

Recognising an opportunity

The opportunity to embark on a supportive one-to-one relationship may arise out of another relationship. It may, for example, grow slowly with the development of a shared interest between a group member and a youth leader, or else present itself from a chance remark during a conversation about careers with a personal adviser from a Connexions partnership. A young person is much more likely to talk about their real worries when they have had time to get to know and trust an 'outsider', such as in a mentoring relationship (see below).

However the opportunity arises, engaging in a supportive one-to-one relationship based on mutual respect may be the most valuable help available. In the long run it may have more lasting value than practical help or advice. By giving a troubled young person some undivided attention, by taking their concerns seriously and by staying alongside through a difficult period they may come to realise that you can be trusted. If you are not overwhelmed by them or their difficulties and if you continue to keep in contact even when they test you out, then perhaps you really care. From this experience they may learn how to relate, to be able to voice their problems and to extend trust. Even if you do not have the training, skill or expertise to give the specialist help required you can provide the stepping-stone of emotional experience which enables the adolescent to accept and use such help in due course. Thus, the most troubled young person who may have otherwise rejected or shied away from help may, eventually, be able to ask for professional advice or engage in counselling or treatment.

Aims for the helping relationship

Unlike a counselling relationship (which may focus on particular problems and enable change in attitudes, perspectives and behaviour), this first helping relationship may have the following general aims:

- Containing the young person's anxiety.
- Safeguarding their best interests.
- Encouraging self-respect, self-control and independence.

Containing anxiety

An adolescent with problems may have overwhelming anxieties. These can be so incapacitating that they can longer function normally in some situations. If they feel anger, shame, guilt or inadequacy they will be desperately looking for cues about how you view them. Your first responses will be important, whether it is a first meeting or when being trusted with a confidence. If you allow yourself to show shock or respond negatively, your reaction may be interpreted as either rejection or that the problem is so enormous or terrible that you cannot cope with hearing it. Either will confirm their terrible feelings about themselves and may increase depression and despair, so that they are unable to look for other help.

If you remain relaxed, empathic and demonstrate the qualities and skills which are discussed in Chapter 3, then the young person may experience some relief in finding that the emotions that they are unloading are not beyond your capacity. You have not immediately collapsed or brushed them off. What is more, by staying with them, you are signalling that they do not deserve the blame or shame that they are heaping on themselves.

Sometimes an 'enormous problem' actually sounds rather trivial in the telling. Just keep in mind the world from their perspective and do not judge what you have heard from your own world view. Remember that anything which is causing anxiety for the young person is worthy of your full attention and sensitivity. Anything less in the first instance will break the trust. Putting things into perspective may be helpful later, but should not be the initial response.

By listening, responding gently and working to understand their perspective you will be absorbing or containing some of their anxiety. In this way you provide some immediate emotional support.

The best interests of the individual

By adolescence an individual will have experienced quite a few relationships with adults. They may have ongoing relationships with parents, with adult family members, teachers and others in authority. With all of these people the relationship has been unequal in that the adult has held most of the power and control, albeit, hopefully, with the child's welfare and well being in mind.

Unlike these adults, the youth worker or mentor may offer a more independent relationship than those whose own interests or reputations are affected by the behaviour or achievements of the adolescent. This relationship is not imbued with family values, loyalties, jealousies and all the other emotional family dynamics. Thus praise is also particularly welcomed and valued because it appears untainted by emotional bonds (Darling et al., 1994). In addition an outsider who is not familiar with the young person's background will not be affected by knowledge of past history, except through the reporting of their client. Thus power and authority may be less obvious in this relationship and the young person may experience less inequality than in other relationships with adults. This will be more so where the youth worker is also only a little older than the client.

The youth worker should also be aware of the young person's vulnerabilities. Are child protection issues relevant? Is this lad likely to be bullied if he joins the group? Will this girl's parents allow her to participate? The youth worker must also consider their own motives. For example, if they are a sports club leader supporting a young protégé are they considering the best interests of that individual or are they thinking about enhancing the reputation of the club? These issues are addressed more fully in Chapters 2 and 3.

During time together, ideally, the focus can be directed on the young person and their best interests. This may be a first opportunity to express ideas and personal opinions to an objective outsider. They may feel able to make some choices about their activities. The interest and support of this independent outsider might encourage feelings of self-worth.

Encouraging self-respect and independence

The youth worker can encourage feelings of self-respect by demonstrating that they value the young person and hold a good opinion of their positive potential. Most of us derive much of our self-concept, how we see ourselves, from the feedback we receive from others. Adolescents care about the responses, reactions and opinions of individuals whom they respect. In naturally occurring relationships:

> When a particular teacher or coach becomes important to an adolescent, it is either because the adolescent sees in that person qualities the adolescent admires and wants to emulate or because the person holds a vision of the adolescent that the adolescent wants to share.
>
> Darling, Hamilton and Niego, 1994: p229.

If the adolescent is helped to recognise their own potential as reflected by their mentor, then they may be able to work together towards the same goal. At the same time the mentor can act as a role model.

Sometimes it is a crisis which acts as a catalyst to propel a young person into seeking help. The youth worker can provide the time and place to discuss the events and circumstances leading to the crisis and to think about possible ways forward. Together the options may be considered. Then the young person may be able to select an option, so finding their own path. In the future they may seek similar support from peers who are equally able to discuss the options and allow them to decide.

The youth worker needs to know when to stand back and let the individual get on with it. Although it is easy for the helpful adult to take over, it is more constructive to allow the young person to take some decisions, to make some mistakes along the way and to learn from them. It may be easier for the outsider than for the parent when decision-making includes an element of risk. However life is about weighing up advantages and risks as, for example, when deciding on places to live, jobs to take, money to be borrowed or partnerships to cement. Without early experience of decision-making and taking responsibility for the results, the adolescent is less well prepared for adulthood.

Like a good parent the youth worker needs to be there if things go wrong. Then is the time to offer more support, without any hint of 'I told you so!' or 'if only you had asked!', but to help them back onto their feet and, when they are ready, encourage them to go off again! That is the path to independence.

Relationships develop slowly

For the young person who has previously found most adults to be unreliable or insensitive a relationship may be difficult to establish. For example: a young person who has been in local authority care may have built up defence barriers and be fearful or resistant to making yet another relationship which will prove to be disappointing or hurtful. If time is limited then an attempt at a close relationship may be more damaging than helpful. If one of you is likely to be moving on in a few weeks then acknowledge that you can only talk about some present difficulties with short-term solutions. Do not try to find out much about past experiences.

Allow plenty of time for the trust to build gradually. Let the young person move at their own pace and keep their distance whether physical, communicative or emotional, until they feel able to share more. Just remain open, non-judgmental and patient. If there is an imposed role such as mentor-mentee which has brought you together you might acknowledge that it is difficult to really get to know one another. You may be tested by the most fearful or needy young person. You will have to muster all your own self-esteem and life experience to remain non-confrontational and emotionally available, but patience may be rewarded.

This case study illustrates a relationship that developed slowly and unevenly over more than a year. Initially Robert was reluctant to engage. Despite early

---

Case study: Robert

13 year old Robert was a popular lad who could make his friends laughs. Ajay, the youth project worker, was pleased to have such a lively group member. However, when the young people broke into subgroups to get on with indoor activities, the people with whom Robert was working never seemed to accomplish anything. They always needed extra attention from Ajay to keep them on track and he soon realised that Robert, with his clowning about, was the distracting influence.

Ajay found that drawing Robert away from the group allowed the others to focus on their task, but Robert was not comfortable with being singled out. Ajay suspected that literacy difficulties could be part of the problem but he could not be sure. During the winter months Robert's attendance was erratic and Ajay was irritated by his behaviour when he did attend. On one occasion Robert was so disruptive that Ajay had to respond firmly and this resulted in Robert storming off.

However Robert returned for the summer outdoor activities. He was enthusiastic and, though clumsy, he participated fully. Ajay made the most of this by encouraging Robert, praising his efforts and generally talking to him quite often. Extrovert Robert was surprisingly reserved when given the chance to talk about himself.

The following autumn Robert attended few meetings but he arrived one December evening with a direct request. He had an application form to complete and he reckoned Ajay could help. Ajay was delighted and arranged a time when they could tackle the lengthy form. After a couple of short sessions working on the form, Ajay was more convinced that Robert had literacy problems and, emboldened by the slowly building trust, Ajay raised the subject. Immediately Robert bristled and rejected the suggestion. Their session ended rather abruptly. To Ajay's surprise Robert turned up at the following meeting and indicated that his writing and spelling were getting him down and that he wouldn't mind talking about it, just to Ajay. The patient approach paid off and Ajay eventually introduced Robert to a local literacy support scheme.

difficulties when rejection would have been an easier option, Ajay managed to maintain an open friendly attitude towards Robert and to give him attention and personal encouragement. This fostered enough trust for Robert to ask Ajay when he really needed help. Once the relationship was established, the real difficulties could be tackled. Ajay was the stepping-stone to further help.

Mentoring

While many one-to-one relationships with young people are only short or occasional, longer, regular relationships, such as in mentoring, can be of great value. Mentoring is an age-old concept. It is described by Homer in the Greek classic: 'The Odyssey', where Odysseus, who was leaving for war, asked Mentor to be the experienced and trusted adviser to his son Telemachus, (National Mentoring Network, 2002). The emphasis was on nurturing the young man's mental development as a patriot-warrior rather than his technical skills, (Gibb, 1997). Through the centuries mentoring has been used in the work-place, such as in the apprentice-master relationship, where an older, experienced individual provides long-term one-to-one advice and guidance for a younger person.

The mentoring system has been used too by youth workers in the United States since the Big Brothers/Big Sisters Programme was introduced in 1904 (Porteus, 2001). Typical US mentoring programmes 'were designed to help disadvantaged youth to gain skills and responsibility by placing them with caring and competent adult volunteers' (Jaffe, 1998: p226). Research showed that mentoring relationships worked best when the mentor and the young person worked together on a project towards shared goals (Darling, Hamilton and Niego, 1994). The successful mentors were those who wanted to teach something and focused on activities which were more than just getting to know the young person. As they found: 'Ironically, relationships were built when building a relationship was *not* the main purpose for getting together' (Darling et al., 1994: p228). They also pointed out that sustaining mentoring relationships could be more difficult than anticipated at the outset due to the usual barriers that naturally arise in adolescent-adult relationships.

Many of the UK government directed mentoring programmes, introduced in the late 1990s, have been particularly directed towards young people who are disadvantaged, underachieving in education or 'at risk' of offending. Porteous (2001) described a range of mentoring schemes including one targeted at young people from ethnic minorities where a mentor of the same ethnic identity and gender acts as a role model. On other schemes volunteer mentors worked with young offenders, meeting regularly, accompanying them on trips and helping them with schoolwork. Underlying all these programmes has been the intention that the young person can benefit from the positive relationship with the mentor, by having the undivided attention of an adult who was positive, supportive and took their concerns seriously. Having evaluated some of the schemes Porteous stressed that where the young people had entrenched problems and were already disillusioned, progress could be very limited. He concluded that while mentoring is known to enhance personal development, it may not be able to correct problematic behaviour.

While recognising that even very small changes are beneficial, the mentor needs to retain a realistic perspective about their role. Where an adolescent needs additional professional help the mentor may be able to initiate that, while maintaining commitment and continuing to work on their shared goals. Only in future years may the young person come to recognise the value of the mentoring relationship. After all how many of us recognise the significant teacher, coach or mentor affecting our life-path until many years afterwards?

While mentoring is not counselling, it can be an opportunity to be emotionally responsive. The mentor needs to find the balance between working with the young person within the structure of a scheme, giving encouragement and praising achievement, while at the same time being receptive to their concerns and alert to the circumstances which may be blocking success.

Making it acceptable to seek help again

One of the most valuable legacies of a first positive relationship with an adult outside the family is the experience of being recognised as an individual of worth. One helpful relationship can encourage a young person to approach other people; a problem, once perceived as too terrible to mention, becomes one that can be talked about in the right circumstances. Making new relationships with adults may become easier and the young person may seek further adult help with less fear of being controlled or patronised.

Further reading

Porteous, D. (2001) Mentoring. In Factor, F., Chauhan, V. and Pitts, J. (Eds.) *The RHP Companion to Working with Young People.* Lyme Regis: Russell House Publishing.

Useful website

National Mentoring Network: www.nmn.org.uk

Chapter 2

Responsible Working Practice

To provide effective support for adolescents, the helper needs an organised way of working, some professional guidelines and, most important of all, good support. This chapter considers:

- supervision
- confidentiality
- record keeping
- some ethical dilemmas
- boundaries

By acting in a competent and professional manner the helper protects both the interests of the young person and themselves.

Before rushing in to help a needy adolescent, the aspiring helper needs to consider their personal and professional resources so that they can work in a responsible manner:

The rescuer who jumps selflessly, but thoughtlessly, into the rushing river to rescue a drowning person may drown too.

The rescuer who throws a lifebuoy or who jumps in only when tied to a team of supporters on the riverbank may be able to affect a rescue.

Before embarking on helping relationships, there are preparations to be made.

Consultant supervision

Initiating and maintaining a relationship with a difficult or demanding adolescent can be emotionally draining. Providing support for a young person with a confused understanding of right and wrong may lead to moral dilemmas. While supporting a young person the helper might experience a crisis or difficult period in their own personal life which impacts on the helping relationship. For these reasons, and many more, the helper needs regular support from another professional which is best delivered in 'supervision'.

Supervision is a process of regular consultation between the helper (here the youth worker or mentor) and another person, the supervisor, who is usually a professional with experience in the same or similar field of work and who primarily provides support for the helper. Ideally the supervisor is an independent professional and not the helper's manager with direct responsibility for the work and the way it is done. While a manager normally has to consider the clients, staff and the organisation, and may be under pressure from above to increase 'working together' and/or achieve more 'accredited outcomes' – the supervisor may focus solely on supporting the helper and their professional well being.

On a regular basis, (weekly, fortnightly or monthly) the supervisor and helper (supervisee) meet to discuss and reflect on the helper's relationships with individual adolescents and on other issues affecting their work such as resources and the impact of other people and institutions. After reflecting with their supervisor, the youth worker may construct a different perspective of a young person's situation, leading perhaps to more intensive work, or to a new approach. By discussing individual cases in confidence there is an opportunity to monitor and evaluate the helping relationship in an environment where it is safe to discuss dilemmas and shortcomings as well as successes. This enables the youth worker (scout leader, sports coach or mentor) to develop skills and understanding and so this, indirectly, supports the clients.

Consultant supervision has three functions, (Leigh, 1998). Firstly it is restorative, providing support and encouragement. Secondly it is formative, in that teaching can take place alongside the case discussion, so that new approaches and skills can be developed. Thirdly it is normative meaning that it monitors the ethical considerations (see below). The supervisor can check that the helper is working within their own limitations and is competent to deal with the situations they face. If not, they can be helped to refer to someone with relevant expertise. The supervisor can help to monitor the caseload, checking that the youth worker is not taking on more than they can effectively manage or becoming physically or emotionally exhausted. Sometimes a supervisor may recognise that a relationship has become inappropriate and suggest an ending for the benefit of one or both parties. The supervisor primarily nurtures the youth worker, but by doing so indirectly also looks after the best interests of that worker's individual clients too.

The institutional context of the work can also be discussed in supervision:

Pat works for a church where various forms of contraception are considered against the religious teachings. She is concerned that a young woman, whom she is supporting currently, is regularly risking pregnancy. What options does she have?

Mentor Dan has found that David is cheating on his youth justice Supervision Order programme because it is just too difficult for him to conform. How does he tell the institution without making matters worse for David?

As an independent outsider the supervisor can help the youth worker to reflect on the goals of the institution and the best interests of the individual. The youth worker may wish to initiate change but fear creating difficulties with colleagues or facing inflexible management. The supervisor may suggest ways to introduce new ideas in a non-threatening manner or to acknowledge that nothing can be done for the time being. Sometimes an astute supervisor recognises that employers are unaware of the good work being done and can help the youth worker to provide full reports of their work so that their worth can be recognised and appreciated.

Getting supervision

In the professions of counselling and psychotherapy supervision is a requirement, not a luxury, and it should be the same in all areas of youth work. Consultant supervision for all youth workers was discussed as long ago as the 1960s and the Youth Service Association provided training for supervisors (Marchant, 1989). However many youth workers still only receive supervision during training. Even organisations with good line management may not provide independent consultant supervision. The youth worker or mentor should ask their organisation to consider providing supervision.

To find a supervisor, approach someone whom you trust and respect, and who has experience of working with young people but is not currently involved with your own organisation or area. Ideally this person will be a trained supervisor. Otherwise, an experienced youth or community worker, who has experienced supervision or a secondary school teacher with experience of reflecting on practice with colleagues, may fill the role. If there is no obvious candidate, ask trainers or colleagues for recommendations. This is a professional relationship and, unless both of you are working as volunteers; the consultant will usually expect payment. In an ideal world your employer should pay the fee. However you should benefit sufficiently to feel that it is worthwhile to pay for yourself.

An example of supervision

McKay (1989) describes the process of non-managerial supervision as collaboration between two equal partners with the supervisee acting as the 'explorer'; and the supervisor as the 'observer'. The supervisee brings issues of concern and discusses how to deal with a situation. The supervisor may put this into context and perhaps show how this could be a pattern of behaviour. As the independent observer, the supervisor may point out issues in the youth/youth worker relationship that the worker has been too involved to recognise. (See Case Study Example, page 15.)

Ethical considerations

Although youth workers cannot be pre-prepared for every ethical dilemma that may arise, it is worth considering some of the more common areas of difficulty. This section aims just to raise awareness. Specific issues should be aired in supervision.

Case study: Supervision

Jenny, an experienced youth leader, ran a youth club in local authority premises. She consulted her supervisor about 14 year old Natalie. Natalie had previously been an enthusiastic member but now was disrupting activities and setting a poor example to younger members. Jenny had spoken to Natalie about her behaviour on a couple of occasions. After one 'quiet chat' Natalie's mother, who happened to be a local authority councillor, had phoned to ask why Jenny was 'picking on her daughter'. Jenny felt uncomfortable and concerned.

A week later Natalie managed to sabotage an activity by accidentally breaking a vital piece of equipment. Jenny had another quiet word, trying to understand Natalie's behaviour. By the time she got home there was an answer phone message to ring Natalie's mother immediately. When she phoned back, Natalie's mother defended her daughter's behaviour, in a somewhat bullying way.

In supervision Jenny talked about Natalie and also mentioned that she felt intimidated by the mother. Through discussion she realised that she was particularly worried that if she handled this wrongly, poor reports about her to other councillors could put her in jeopardy of losing funding for the club or even her job.

In partnership Jenny and her supervisor discussed how her concern about Natalie's mother and the associated issues were affecting the way Jenny was reacting to Natalie's behaviour. Was her super-sensitivity being counterproductive? The supervisor observed that Jenny had worked competently with several other difficult fourteen year olds in the past and had been running the group very well for several years. Natalie's mother had been happy for her daughter to join the group.

With this fuller perspective Jenny decided that she would not react so promptly to phone calls from Natalie's mother but would take time to prepare herself to respond adult to adult. She would also ensure that no activities were dependent on Natalie's co-operation, allowing Natalie the space to decide whether to participate, but drawing a firm, prompt boundary if she began to disrupt a programme. After a few weeks Natalie decided that she had outgrown the club. One other girl left with her but the remainder stayed. There were no other repercussions.

A few weeks later Jenny could use a session of supervision to reflect on the experience, to consider what she had learned and to think how she would adapt her practice in the future.

Confidentiality

Information given by a client to a professional worker is often understood to be confidential and not to be divulged to another. However professional relationships are not the same as a person confiding a secret to a friend. While many confidences can be kept, there are occasions when confidentiality should be broken. A youth worker may face a dilemma in deciding whether to keep a confidence and preserve the autonomy of the client or to break the confidence for the greater good of society and possibly the client too, but risk accusations of betrayal and the loss of a trusting relationship.

Morgan and Banks (1999) cite an example which can be summarised as follows:

In an inner city area a youth worker talks to young people about their illegal drug use. He introduces them to the youth centre and to harm reduction strategies. In the course of this he gains information about a local drug dealer. Should the youth worker inform the police? To do so may lead to the arrest, trial, conviction and removal of the dealer from the streets. However this might also jeopardise all the trust and goodwill that he has fostered with the group of young people and they may boycott the successful project.

The youth worker who has some policy guidance from their organisation and a colleague or supervisor to consult will have support in choosing the best course of action.

Regarding confidentiality, there are differences in working practice for professionals in different situations. Sensitive information given to a counsellor by an adult client may remain confidential, while the same information given by a vulnerable adolescent may have to be disclosed.

The youth worker has a duty to protect the individual and also to consider other young people in the community.

The informal nature of some youth worker-adolescent relationships can make the understanding of confidentiality issues more problematic. In formal relationships, the youth worker and young person may set up a contract about meeting and may discuss from the outset how information is to be shared, with whom and for which purpose. In contrast an outreach worker may meet a group of young people in a particular location on one day and the group members may be different at the next meeting. Contact with an individual may begin on a street corner with a conversation developing before the youth worker has time to explain the limits of confidentiality:

Case study: An ethical dilemma

Tom, a young youth worker, mixes easily with a changing group who hang around at the edge of an estate. He knows some of them by name but has never met Mel before. She looks no more than twelve but her behaviour is attention-seeking and full of bravado. Chancing upon her later, she is clearly upset. A few friendly words from him and out tumbles part of a story. He fears that Mel may be a victim of abuse. She has assumed that he is a friend or group member and that what she has said will remain a secret. He has responded genuinely and with empathy but he has not told her that he is a youth worker with duties and responsibilities. If she is not given immediate protection will she come to serious harm before she can help herself? Or is he making some wrong assumptions? Should he tell Social Services? Would anyone do anything useful if he did tell?

The youth worker who has thought through possible situations beforehand may have the presence of mind to talk about the next step whilst still with the young person. Tom might have explained that by talking to him Mel had taken the first steps towards getting help for herself. Together they could talk to a colleague. Even if Mel is reluctant to speak to anyone else, Tom has clearly indicated that he cannot just keep the secret. If he is part of a multi-disciplinary team he may already know the best professionals to contact, perhaps in the local social services team. He will be able to suggest a sensitive approach to Mel and follow up to ensure that the referral is being handled. Alternatively he can devise a plan of action with his supervisor or manager.

Breaking confidentiality

There are circumstances when confidentiality has to be broken for the safety of the client or of other people. Child protection issues or crime may be obvious, such as when a rape is disclosed or when bruises from a beating are shown. However there are many more occasions when the information is far from clear and it is difficult to decide whether to break the confidence.

The legal and ethical issues are complex. The procedures to be followed will be affected by the information involved, the surrounding circumstances and the age of the client. These will affect who is to be told, how and the amount of control the young person may be allowed to exercise in the disclosure.

The youth worker or mentor should seek immediate help from a supervisor, manager or other professional.

The following may help to clarify concerns:

- How serious is the present situation?
- What are the immediate and significant risks to the young person?
- Could anyone else be at risk?
- What are the implications of breaking confidentiality (for the young person, for others and for yourself)?
- What harm could occur if you do **not** break confidentiality?

If you do have a good reason to break confidentiality, then try to limit the negative consequences by thinking about:

- Why you are breaking the confidence.
- Who you will tell.
- What you will tell them.
- What they are likely to do with the information.
- What consequences this will have for the young person and for your relationship with them.

You will need to explain the above to the young person.

Adapted from Sheffield University's Website, 2002.

If no-one is available for consultation, advice may be gained from the following:

- your organisation's head office
- your professional body
- NSPCC helpline: 0808 800 5000
- child protection duty officer at local social services

Child Protection Issues Training

Being well prepared to cope with issues involving child protection is strongly recommended. If your own organisation or local social services / child protection team cannot offer training then contact the NSPCC. They offer a variety of training courses on child protection awareness including inexpensive distance learning courses.

To find out more: www.nspcc.org.uk/inform/CH_Training.asp

Breaking the law

Whether to turn a blind eye to 'minor' infringements of the law rather than jeopardise a good relationship is another frequently occurring dilemma:

> *The young-looking 18 year old admits to buying a child's fare travel ticket so that she can afford to visit her grandfather once a week.*
>
> *A lad is seen putting some badly needed food under his coat.*

It is easy to empathise and to ignore this behaviour. However this is theft and to collude is to give the wrong message. The youth worker or mentor may be the only respected adult in an individual's life who is capable of setting them a moral standard. This could just be the top of a slippery slope and timely intervention is needed. The youth worker should address this behaviour immediately. It is important to explain why this is theft, the consequences of being caught and prosecuted and the concept that there is no such thing as victimless crime. (Theft affects shop-owners and leads to price rises for everyone else.) Even if the advice is ignored there will be no perception that the behaviour is accepted by the youth worker.

Where your organisation or agency has an agreed policy regarding the law (e.g. for under-age sex, cannabis smoking, etc.) keep to it. Where there is no such policy uphold the current law, whatever your personal feelings. If you have a professional body, join it and familiarise yourself with their code of ethics. If you find yourself in a quandary consult your supervisor or manager or contact your professional body. Take legal advice from a professionally qualified legal adviser.

Moral conflicts

Ethical dilemmas arise in many forms. Trying to support an adolescent with a disability to gain independence may be an uphill struggle against adult expectations and concerns about health and safety; discussing moral values with a group of young refugees who are being badly treated by the local community may involve confronting prejudices on all sides. Values held by the youth worker may also conflict with some of the personal, family or cultural values of the young people with whom they are working.

In *The Art of Youth Work,* Kerry Young (1999) describes and quotes the dilemmas experienced by a range of youth workers in the UK. These include:

Allowing space for young people with learning difficulties to talk about sexual relationships and contraception, while knowing that their parents would disapprove.

Working for a youth service in Northern Ireland with a focus on cross-community work and political education, which conflicted with sectarian views held by community leaders and parents.

The hypocrisy of spending an evening talking with adolescents about the harmful effects of drugs and then going off to relax with colleagues over drinks in the pub.

Another example from Imam (1999) describes:

The difficulty of mediating between a mother and daughter who were members of an Asian women's group. While the daughter felt that she had the right to marry a young man from another culture, the widowed mother feared the effect on her own position and that of her other daughters within their traditional community.

These examples can only give a flavour of the ethical dilemmas that may arise. The youth worker is best prepared if they have given themselves the opportunity to examine where they stand on the different issues and then to look at them from other perspectives. Do they agree with the fundamental principles of the organisation for which they are working? Can divergent opinions be squared? Where an adolescent discovers that they can no longer subscribe to the principles of the organisation, is there an appropriate route for a satisfactory leaving, with the door remaining ajar? Again supervision may provide time, space and invaluable support.

Record keeping

It is good working practice to keep basic written details regarding the young people with whom you are working and some notes of your work together. Such information can be useful for purposes of making a referral, contacting parents or guardians, for supervision or just for reminding yourself of issues to be considered and progress being made. It will be invaluable if the nature of your relationship or your professionalism is ever brought into question, or even into a court of law.

If your organisation does not provide a form, you may wish to devise your own. Basic details for each young person would include:

- full name
- address
- date of birth
- school, college or employment
- name of parents or guardians
- GP's name address and telephone number (optional – for emergency use only)

Notes might include outline of problems. Jot down key areas of discussion and even key phrases used by your client. When you decide to make an intervention, note down the reasons that have led you to taking that decision and add the evidence to back it up. Trainee counsellors may also want to put down some feelings. However do remember that anything written can potentially be seen by another, including your colleagues, your employer and your client. Only put into writing what you will be comfortable with your client reading.

Disclosure

If information about the young person is to be shared with a third party, discuss specifically to whom you will talk and what you can and cannot say. Then get their signed permission. For example:

> *I give permission for Jan Roberts to talk to my teacher Mr Hazan about my health problem. This is to explain why I am often late for class and why my work has been poor recently.*

This should then be signed and dated.

Ensuring confidentiality of records

All records and notes must be stored securely, preferably in a locked filing cabinet. If you belong to an organisation or have a colleague who would take over your work if you were 'knocked down by a bus' then someone should know how to access your records. It is best not to take folders of confidential notes when out working, as bags and brief cases can disappear from under one's nose and cause embarrassment later. Some jotted notes or brief tape-recorded notes made immediately after a meeting, using just a client reference number or initials, may be sufficient to jog your memory for later 'writing up'.

Data Protection Act

Storing data on computers or manually is governed by the Data Protection Act 1998. Individuals have a right to see information held about them. Anyone wishing to store client details about others should find out about the Data Protection Principles and whether they need to register individually by contacting the office of the Data Protection Registrar, Wycliff House, Water Lane, Winslow, Cheshire, SK9 5 AF. Tel: 01625 545700.

Why set boundaries?

Boundaries are for the benefit and protection of both the young person and the supporter:

> *Youth worker Liz was exhausted and went to bed early, so the phone ringing at 10.30 p.m. woke her with a start. It was 13 year old Sam whom she had met at the club earlier in the evening. 'Yes, she had given her home number and said that she could ring at any time but she hadn't meant..."*

> *Mentor Darren gave the teenager a hug to show that he understood. He was stunned when she returned a passionate embrace...*

> *Lette had been sitting with the tearful adolescent for an hour and a half. She was not sure how to bring this to an end without making matters worse.*

Situations such as these can arise when a needy young person finds a sympathetic helper and where the boundaries of the relationship are unclear. Since this supporter–young person relationship is very different from a close friendship, where support might be expected at all times and physical contact is acceptable, it is the responsibility of the helper to maintain boundaries for the benefit of both parties. Some boundaries need to be made explicit such as times for meeting and who to contact in an emergency. The youth worker can use their discretion as to whether or when boundaries regarding behaviour need to be voiced.

As establishing boundaries is an important part of all helping relationships and particularly those with vulnerable clients, most local authorities run short courses on working within boundaries when dealing with child protection and attending such a course is recommended (see above). The issues relating to boundaries which are discussed below include:

- time and place
- behaviour
- physical contact and sexual relationships

Establishing time and place boundaries

In formal relationships, such as mentoring, a regular appointment at a fixed location may be dictated by the organisers. However at the first meeting it may still be helpful for the mentor and mentee to discuss exact times for beginning subsequent meetings and the length of time to be spent together. Both parties then need to agree that they will start punctually and that the mentor will be responsible for bringing their meeting to an end on time. How and when to make contact in case of a meeting difficulty or other crisis can also be agreed.

In informal relationships, where others may be vying for attention, the youth worker may respond immediately:

We can take ten minutes now.

...or give a clear indication:

Straight after the meeting ends, we could have 20 minutes to talk about this.

The suitability of a meeting place should also be considered. It should have sufficient privacy for others not to overhear conversation or to observe the details of any work. On the other hand, for the good of both parties, it should not be so private that there could be accusations of impropriety. Ideally another adult colleague should be nearby and with easy access but out of immediate earshot.

For more details on establishing time, place and contact boundaries, see Chapter 4.

Boundaries of behaviour

The boundaries of behaviour which are acceptable within the youth worker/ adolescent relationship may be based on past experience and guided by organisational rules. Everyday language for some adolescents is peppered with swear words. Within reason the youth worker may feel that they do not need to raise this as an issue. However, if they find that some words or phrases distract them or make them feel very uncomfortable then they must raise it and explain what is not acceptable whilst they are working together.

Abusive or aggressive behaviour should never be tolerated. Racist or sexist language or opinions should also be confronted. The worker should explain and make it clear that they will have to end the relationship if the boundaries are overstepped.

Behaviour that is always unacceptable may need to be spelled out at the beginning. Youngsters will accept ground rules such as no smoking, no possession of drugs or other illegal items. This is for the helper's legal protection as well as that of the young person.

Upholding the boundaries

The youth worker must uphold the boundaries that they have set out if they are to keep the respect of their clients. Young people do test out boundaries. While some transgressions are due to forgetfulness or stress, others are deliberate. Do not turn a blind eye and compromise yourself.

- If the boundary break is minor:
    - point it out
    - ask for an apology
    - accept the apology
- If the violation is serious
    - focus on the situation rather than the person so that you can stay as emotionally neutral and non-judgemental as possible.

I have just noticed that you have...with you today. You may remember that when we first met I explained that while we were together we had to observe certain rules. One of the rules is being broken and this puts me in a difficult situation. I have to end this meeting today which will give you the opportunity to...I shall have to notify...I look forward to seeing you next...at...

or

This behaviour is unacceptable because...I need to consider whether we can continue to work together and I shall need time to do this. I or someone from... will get in touch with you. Meanwhile we shall draw this session to an end now.

Remain open and straightforward and do your best to control any outward signs of anger, frustration or fear. The transgression may have to be reported to your organisation or another agency (e.g. social services, youth offending team) and it should certainly be discussed in supervision. If there is a next meeting it may be appropriate to talk about why the last session ended abruptly.

Physical contact and personal boundaries

Sexual relationships between doctors and their patients, therapists and their clients, teachers and their pupils are all strictly prohibited by professional codes of conduct – but they still occasionally happen. The vulnerable client seeking advice and support finds a sympathetic professional on whom they can depend. The professional gains from the heady mixture of power and flattery and boundaries are broken. Even where both parties are consenting single adults the short-term gains are certainly outweighed by the long-term consequences for both parties. If the relationship becomes public the professional is very likely to lose their job and professional standing and so not work again.

Occasionally the innocent professional is accused of indiscretion by a malicious, unbalanced, dissatisfied or disappointed client and the ensuing suspension and investigation also have devastating effects.

If professionals working in structured work settings with fixed practice codes relating to physical contact with patients and clients can find themselves in grave difficulty, then the youth worker working in informal settings with vulnerable youngsters needs to protect themselves:

- One-to-one meetings with a young person should take place within calling distance of a colleague. (It is also helpful for the client to know that your working practice demands that it is for their safety too that your meeting is not secret.)
- If part of a team, inform colleagues of ongoing one-to-one work for your own protection.
- If working alone, inform your supervisor of ongoing one-to-one work.

In residential settings whether it is a weekend away or a more permanent venue, the bedroom is often the quiet room where the lonely or alienated young person is taking refuge. Again it is prudent to think first and act before embarking on a long conversation. If there really is nowhere more suitable to talk, let someone else know where you are and who you are with and suggest that they put their head round the door after a few minutes. Such chaperoning may sound very old-fashioned but it is sound practice.

Physical contact can be another area of difficulty. Avoid physical touching. It can be misinterpreted.

While no touching should be the rule, in some teaching or coaching situations close proximity is required and contact occurs. Whether it is the adjusting of a safety harness or teaching reading skills to compensate for dyslexia, the adolescent with racing hormones can misinterpret the touch. Again steer clear of individual sessions or put safeguards in place first. A vulnerable adolescent with a 'crush' may not see your well-intentioned help from the same perspective. It is up to the youth worker or mentor to think about the personal boundaries and keep them in place (child protection awareness training is relevant, see above).

Ensuring personal safety of the helper

So far this chapter has focused on professional vulnerability, but physical vulnerability must also be carefully considered. Youth workers must be careful not to put themselves at risk of assault, injury or other harm. When working with a young person, sit between them and the door so that you have control of the exit. If the helper feels under threat, they should leave immediately.

Consider whether it is safe to work alone in a particular area. When working alone, always inform others of where you are working, when you should be expected back. Clock out and clock in, agreeing who should be informed if you are not back when expected. Outreach and detached workers should take special care when working in the community. Sound advice can be found in Kaufman (2001).

Setting up responsible working practice

Ideally, before beginning to work with young people, all the issues in this chapter should be considered and all arrangements and systems should be in place. In addition the aspiring youth worker should undertake some training: much can be gained even from short courses.

Further reading

Banks, S. (1999) *Ethical Issues in Youth Work*. London: Routledge.

Kaufman, S. (2001) Detached Youth Work. In Factor, F., Chauhan, V. and Pitts, J. (Eds.) *The Russell House Companion to Working with Young People*. Lyme Regis: Russell House Publishing.

Wheal, A. (1998) *Adolescence: Positive Approaches for Working with Young People*. Lyme Regis: Russell House Publishing.

Chapter 3

Interpersonal Skills: Key Qualities, Prejudices and Communication Skills

This chapter describes the personal qualities and skills brought by the youth worker into a supportive relationship. Key qualities are defined and ways to recognise and consider personal prejudices are discussed. The final section discusses verbal and non-verbal communication skills.

Key interpersonal qualities

Anyone working successfully with adolescents may instinctively be using most of the key interpersonal qualities as described by Dr Carl Rogers, the American founder of person-centred counselling or psychotherapy (Thorne, 1990). These qualities encapsulate the positive attitude needed to initiate and maintain a helpful relationship with another individual. Similar lists can be found both in books which describe positive ways of working with adolescents (Adams and Gullotta, 1983; Wheal, 1998) and in books teaching counselling skills (Egan, 1990). To develop a supportive relationship the following should be demonstrated:

- **Respect**: valuing the young person for who they are, including differences of culture, ability and sexual orientation.
- **Trust**: focusing on the young person's needs, in a way that is under control and safe. Never taking advantage of the young person's vulnerability. Treating the young person's feelings with sensitivity.
- **Empathy**: developing an understanding of some of the young person's feelings and experiences (imagine standing in their shoes) so as to gain an insight into their world and to see life from their perspective.
- **Genuineness**: not putting on a false self but acting true to oneself. Being open and spontaneous in the relationship while having genuine concern for the young individual.
- **Warmth**: showing care, while keeping within professional boundaries.
- **Confidentiality**: agreeing that what is said within the relationship will not be disclosed to another without specific permission (but subject to certain limits, see Chapter 2).
- **Patience**: allowing the young person to proceed at their own pace.

Many of these qualities may already be exercised in everyday relationships. However, most of them can benefit from reconsideration and conscious practice.

Confidentiality needs additional consideration as it has legal and safety implications (see Chapters 2 and 4).

Learning about oneself

Before considering how to support others from diverse backgrounds, each of us needs to think about our own background, assumptions and perspectives. These influence our approach to others.

In addition to our genetic inheritance, each of us is a product of our family and cultural background. These give context to our lives, shaping our experiences and our expectations. Before working with others we each need to look at ourselves and perhaps question the openness or flexibility of our own perspectives. Personal reflection can be useful.

Recognising prejudices

Imagine an exhausting week working with young people:

- An 18 year old girl needs help to find a refuge.
- A young asylum seeker is getting hassled by his neighbours.
- A young single mother is at the end of her tether.

You have managed to contain all these crises and provide support. Then on Friday, at 3.30 p.m., just before your free weekend, a young person calls in at your drop-in centre. How do you respond to:

- Rupert, a public schoolboy, who is worried about his acne?
- Melissa, a doctor's daughter whose exam grades are too low for entry to medical school?

Do you:
a) Spend a few minutes commiserating and reassuring. Having heard that the middle-class youngster is living at home, send them off with some words of comfort.
b) Suggest they pop in the following week if no-one else has been able to help – as you are unable to see them now.
c) Listen and encourage them to talk about themselves before you decide how to respond.

If some problems are of lesser concern, from whose perspective are you judging?

If you have chosen option c) you might hear that Rupert's acne is only part of the problem. He is being bullied, but he can't tell his depressed widowed father. He is contemplating suicide.

You are the first person that Melissa can talk to because you are a stranger. Her parents have been nice enough about her failure, but they have no idea about how desperate she is really feeling. She is cutting herself and throwing up after every meal.

The problem that appears to be only of minor significance to the listener, 'just one of life's little hiccups', may be the signal of a much deeper problem or may assume gigantic proportions for the individual involved.

We all have prejudices but we may not always recognise them. Sometimes we hold beliefs about people who are different from ourselves out of ignorance or fear or just thoughtlessness. Unless we are challenged we may hang on to the beliefs, unconsciously acting detrimentally towards the individual who is different.

Considering our work with colleagues and supervisors is a way of looking at our prejudices – although this won't work if we share the same views. Participating in a short course for counselling or relationship skills can be an effective method of learning about oneself.

Sometimes we learn when we find that our assumptions have been wrong:

The woman in headscarf and overalls, cleaning the hospital kitchen...is a qualified engineer.

At the station the blind man asking for directions...is a television producer.

The student who is graduating with a good university degree in English...is dyslexic.

What assumptions do we make about people before we know them? What presumptions do we have about people with certain disabilities, people riding in Rolls Royces, ex-prisoners?

First we each need to question our own assumptions and counter our individual prejudices. When working with others each of us needs to acknowledge that there are differences, even if it is only an age difference. (Though with every individual relationship there are likely to be many other differences.) Only then can we prepare to learn from the young person about the world from their individual perspective. We need to recognise and be sensitive to issues and to behaviour which may make them feel uncomfortable. Only then can we work alongside them effectively.

How are we perceived?

Another consideration is how we may be perceived by others. Do we need to make changes in ourselves to be acceptable and trusted by the individuals with whom we are planning to work? This does not involve pretending to be what we are not, but we may need to think about appropriate style of appearance and clothing.

The way in which we communicate will affect the perceptions and the responses of the young people we aim to support.

Helpful communication skills

Different aspects of communication need to be considered. These include body language as well as the words that are spoken, for both affect the nature of relationship. To initiate a trusting relationship, think about:

- non-verbal communication (body language)
- listening skills

- responding to demonstrate that you are listening and that you understand
- avoiding pitfalls

Non-verbal communication

Be fully aware of your body language. This non-verbal communication can indicate your interest, concern and respect; it may also reveal feelings you do not wish to disclose. Talking warmly and listening empathetically to a young person will not be helpful if your body language is expressing your own mounting anxiety or fear, or even disgust. You need to think about your facial expression and other body cues.

To demonstrate that you are attending with full concentration, Gerard Egan (1990) suggests a useful acronym **S-O-L-E-R.** As this was originally written for trainee counsellors working in a western culture, youth workers in the UK must allow for cultural differences and adapt accordingly. When starting to talk to a young person position yourself:

S – Squarely:	facing squarely towards the young person. This signals attention with one's whole being, not just with the face.'I am fully involved with you.' However, chairs facing directly may be perceived as confrontational or threatening, so sit at an angle. If a table is unavoidable, sit across a corner.
O – Open:	adopt an open posture by not crossing your arms or legs. This is a welcoming stance, indicating 'I want to hear what you have to say!'
L – Lean:	lean or incline slightly towards the young person, again indicating interest.
E – Eye contact:	keeping eye contact with the client also indicates listening. By observing others you can see that the person speaking may look away while they are talking but they look back at the listener as they finish indicating that it is their turn to respond. (But be aware that direct eye contact is inappropriate in some Eastern cultures.)
R – Relaxed:	remaining relatively relaxed though alert will indicate that you can cope with what you are being told. You are concerned but you are not showing any anxiety that you may be feeling. Nor are you getting irritated, fidgety or bored.

Other non-verbal responses show that you are attending. Small nods of the head and the occasional 'uh-huh' or 'mmmm' (whatever comes naturally) will encourage a speaker. Initially you may smile a little to be welcoming but then you will need to adjust your expression in response to what they are saying or doing. This will probably come naturally but should be kept at a level which just conveys that you are listening and understanding. Avoid exaggerated facial expressions or gestures by acting normally but remaining aware of the messages you are sending. (For tips on encouraging a young person to begin talking, see Chapter 4.)

Listening

Listening is an active process and is more than just hearing. Take in all that is being communicated by the speaker, both the words and the body language, and try to understand its meaning. Be alert to the language being used, the inflections in voice and gesture and the overall mood of the client. Though your body may look relaxed your mind will be actively processing what you see, hear and feel, so that you become attuned to the young person to whom you are listening. Only then will you begin to understand from their perspective and begin to share the meaning.

Just allowing an individual time and space to talk and paying them undivided attention can be helpful in itself. Do not be tempted to respond too quickly. In our hurried lives time is a luxury. As a person hears themself they may be able to reflect on what they are saying and so understand themselves a little better. When someone pauses, they may not have come to the end. Just wait a little. If your body language is encouraging with S-O-L-E-R then your client may be able to say a little more, expand or describe their feelings more deeply or just go over the ground. They may be saying something out loud for the first time. They may even be able to begin working on their own problem.

Responding verbally

Limit your initial responses, particularly when you are just finding out about the difficulty. Until you have heard the whole of the story you could jump to incorrect conclusions and say the wrong thing. Just respond enough to indicate that you are listening carefully and understanding.

Little prompts such as 'uh-huh' 'go on' 'tell me more' 'so…' all show that you are listening and following. They can be encouraging without interrupting the flow of thought.

There are skilled ways of responding to encourage the speaker, to indicate your understanding and to show that you understand some of how they are feeling and the reasons why. Some of the skills can be very briefly described:

Repetition

A key word or phrase used by the speaker can be repeated. This can be used just to indicate your understanding or used as a question so that you can find out even more. For example:

> Sue: *Ever since he thought he saw me getting close to Matt he has been unpredictable…sort of scary. But meanwhile I still have to work beside him every morning and the teacher says there is no space on the other side of the lab.*
>
> Youth worker: *Unpredictable and sort of scary? (Tell me more.)*

Paraphrasing words

You can use words similar in meaning to those used by the adolescent – but you might use fewer words:

> Tony: *When he said that about my sister and her clothes I just lost my rag and I just hit out – straight at him and even when he went backwards I couldn't stop, even when I saw the blood from his nose like.*
>
> Youth worker: *So when he insulted your sister, you lost your temper and hit him on the nose.*

Again this shows that you are listening and making the effort to understand from his point of view.

Reflecting feelings and words

This involves processing the young person's non-verbal communications, such as gestures and voice tone, as well as their words, to pick up their feelings and reflect them back:

> Lorelle (looking straight at her youth worker with her body tense and her arms tightly folded): *I may as well say now that they found the knife when they searched me. And don't say 'That was stupid', cos I know. I'd had it there a long time cos I hadn't used that bag for ages but I just needed something big as it was raining and I just bunged everything in. 'I hadn't emptied it out or anything so I didn't know it was still there. Honest – but no-one believes me!*
>
> Youth worker: *You are worried whether I will believe that you had the knife in the bag from a long time ago and that you did not take it out on purpose.*

The youth worker understands what the young person has said and how she is feeling at present. This gives Lorelle the opportunity to reflect too. Notice that the youth worker has neither indicated that they believe the client nor have they challenged her. They are just reflecting.

Reflecting is a counselling skill that may be acquired through practice but is not essential for forming a good relationship. It is included here to alert the reader to the different levels of skills that may be developed and practised but these skills can only be briefly mentioned within the scope of this book.

Other books focus in detail on developing counselling skills and the different ways of engaging with individuals in counselling and helping relationships (see end of chapter).

Responding non-verbally

Be aware of your own non-verbal communication signals, particularly after your client has said something new, uncomfortable or upsetting. Keep relaxed and sitting hard on your seat so that you encourage them to continue. Do not allow yourself to show shock or other negative feelings. Do not fold your arms or move back, just try to remain still. Your open response, keeping S-O-L-E-R in mind, can encourage them to feel that they have acted positively in trusting you. Conversely if they sense negativity or disbelief they may decide that they have made a terrible mistake in confiding in you. This may confirm feelings that they are a bad, mad or sad person and that they are beyond help.

By remaining both relaxed and attentive you communicate your ability to listen without being overwhelmed. Your facial expression will indicate your willingness to keep listening so that you can understand more. As mentioned in Chapter 1, you will contain their anxiety if you show that you are strong enough to absorb the emotions that they are unloading and that you are able to stay with them. You also indicate patience by allowing time for both of you to reflect on what has been said. For the young person, just the process of telling may be an enormous relief; your calm and genuine response will provide some immediate emotional support.

Finding out more

If you need to know more you may need to ask a question or two. Beware of leading questions which guide the respondent into answering as you expect or closed questions leading to one word answers such as 'Yes' or 'No'. Open questions beginning 'Who', 'What', 'When' or 'How' will give the young person some scope to expand or explore.

Controlled responding

While these responding skills can be useful to encourage talking and to demonstrate understanding they must be used in moderation. Too much paraphrasing or questioning can be annoying or appear condescending. It is more important to be yourself and allow the young person to do the same.

Don'ts

A helpful list of what to avoid when counselling in health care (Burnard, 1989) can be adapted for working with adolescents:

- Avoid questions beginning with 'Why'.
  Such questions may produce some direct answers but they won't necessarily help the young person to acknowledge true underlying feelings and their source and may lead you to focus on some trivial reasons. For example 'Why are you crying?' 'Because the heel of my shoe broke'.
  Instead 'Perhaps you can tell me a bit about how you are feeling…' may lead to a wider realisation that anger, tears or a feeling of helplessness have been growing over the last few days – ever since…
- Don't use 'should' or 'ought'.
  Advice giving can be unhelpful. If you have a suggestion, phrase it as 'You may want to…' which will give them the option to consider.
- Don't blame anyone – or collude with blaming.
  Firstly there are two or more perspectives to most situations. Remain objective. The young person may need to re-evaluate the situation and may 'about-face'. If you have associated yourself with one definite position they may feel unable to return to you for help.
- Don't automatically compare the client's situation with your own.
  Though two situations may at first seem very similar, there are likely to be

many differences below the surface. Better to listen and focus on them rather than draw attention to your own feelings and experiences. Empathise but don't expect their feelings to be the same as yours. Ask about their feelings.

- Don't invalidate your client's feelings.
  Remarks such as 'Come on, it can't be that bad,' or 'You can't really mean that' or 'You'll soon get over it' are all inappropriate. Instead allow the young person to explore and express their feelings, even those that make you feel uncomfortable.

- Don't try to stop tears.
  Crying can be a relief. Have tissues available and allow the tears to flow. Remain still and quiet, and do not be embarrassed. Acknowledge the relief or the pain and that it is 'okay to cry'.

- **Don't dig too deep!**
  Do not ask questions or otherwise encourage digging into past experiences, hopes and fears, dreams or fantasies. Leave this to trained counsellors, psychologists, psychiatrists and therapists. The danger is that you will uncover difficult feelings or emotional wounds but that you will not have the skill to help them to cope. After talking to you the young person may have to go to a home or school where they feel unsupported. They may brood on what has been uncovered and this may be emotionally damaging or even lead to harmful behaviour.

Instead remain satisfied with what is being said without much prompting. You are not trying to create a dependent relationship. You are helping them to find out that talking can be a positive experience and to take some control. While remembering that your expertise is limited, have the confidence to acknowledge that your present relationship is positive, valuable and giving of your best and is as much as you can reasonably do.

Developing relationship skills

Joining a counselling skills training course is probably the most effective way to develop these skills. Participation in role play and other experiential inter-action provides the opportunity to practise skills in a safe environment, where errors will not be damaging. Trainers and fellow trainees will provide feedback for improving skills and may also encourage reflection on attitudes and perspectives.

Make time, either in training or in supervision, to discuss your aims and goals and the ways in which you are trying to achieve them.

Further reading

Nelson-Jones, R. (1997) *Practical Counselling and Helping Skills: Text and Exercises for the Lifeskills Counselling Model.* London: Cassell.

Chapter 4

Beginnings

This chapter raises the practical issues that need to be addressed at the beginning of a helping relationship. These include:

- setting the time and place boundaries
- explaining the limits of confidentiality
- encouraging the young person to talk
- assessing the situation
- establishing contact arrangements
- keeping the ending in mind

A young person seeking support may approach a stranger such as an agency worker or outreach worker. More often the individual adolescent has already observed the person they have decided to approach and knows a little about them. They may have met informally within a social context (club activity, camp, sports training, music event). Whatever the prior relationship, once the youth worker recognises that the young person may need some one-to-one time, considerations of boundaries and appropriate communication (as discussed in Chapters 2 and 3) should come to the fore.

Setting a professional tone

Early responses by the potential helper may either encourage a relationship or frighten off or disappoint the adolescent. Therefore being alert to an approach and handling it sensitively will have important consequences.

Time and place are usually the first considerations:

- Is this an appropriate time to talk? If not, when?
- Where would be relatively comfortable, discreet but not too private?
- If necessary explain why now is not possible, and then arrange a time and place or method of contact because you would like to respond in a way that will be helpful.

If the present is appropriate:

- then move to the place you have decided upon (notifying someone if you are alone – see Chapter 3).

- seat yourselves.
- focus on the young person.

Introductions, confidentiality and making notes

Introducing yourself by name and very briefly describing your role or job will encourage the young person to give their name too. In informal surroundings you may just be given a nickname, but you also need a first name and family name for your records.

Explain that you would like to keep a note of their name, age and address for your professional records. In most cases you will be able to keep confidential the information that you are told, but just occasionally you are told something that you have to tell your colleagues and others:

Taking an extreme example, if you tell me that you are about to go off to commit a murder, I shall have to tell someone and act to stop you. If you do begin to tell me something that has to be told, I shall warn you and also discuss with you whom we should tell and how we should do it. I shall not go behind your back. However, having said all that, I can usually keep confidences because that is an important part of the work I do.

You may want to make a brief note of name, address and date of birth. Allow the young person to see what you are writing down. Explain that what you are writing will not be secret from them but will be kept and stored carefully in your office and not left around for anyone else to see. (If you are without pen and paper, explain that you will do this later.)

Explaining the initial time boundary

It is helpful from the beginning for the young person to know how long you have together in the initial meeting. If you only have ten minutes before you have to hurry off to an appointment, say so. Then they will not be disappointed or feel rejected when you up and leave before they have completed their story. It may be better to set aside another time. On the other hand if you plan to have 50 minutes together, explain that and so make them aware that there is a finite time with an ending.

Off-putting formalities?

All these preliminaries may sound off-putting and rather formal but in actuality they take only a couple of minutes. They demonstrate that you respect the young person because you are taking them and their concerns seriously and that you will be looking after their best interests. If the youth worker handles these initial procedures in a calm, confident and open manner, the adolescent may begin to feel that their difficult situation is not so unusual for you after all and this may reduce some anxiety or feelings of frustration.

Encouraging the young person to begin

You may need to overcome the adolescent's initial reluctance to speak. A young person who has come to ask for help may not know how to begin; they might suddenly be overwhelmed by the situation or feel that telling anyone is too risky. On the one hand they want to talk about what is troubling them, but on the other hand they are fearful about the reaction they may get. They may be ashamed about what they have to tell...or fearful because they have been building up their hopes about getting help and scared because they may be let down.

Keeping in mind non-verbal communication cues, indicate that you are ready to listen and that they can start from wherever they feel comfortable. You may start by acknowledging how hard it is to begin, with any of the following:

It is often difficult to get started, so just tell me a bit about yourself.

Tell me what has been happening.

It does not matter where you begin.

Tell me one or two things that are concerning you.

- If a story is being told fairly fluently, listen carefully, without interrupting.
- Allow some moments of quiet. It might give thinking space.
- Encourage with nods or 'mmm's and the odd repeated phrase.
- Only prompt and ask questions when the young person needs your help. You should not be an inquisitor, prying for information.
- Do not be tempted to prompt from the beginning with information you have heard from someone else, such as a friend or colleague. Firstly you need to understand the position from this individual's own viewpoint.
- If you have sensitive information from another source, be careful how you disclose what you have heard. It may be wrong! If you really need to clarify the situation, use an indirect approach.

See Chapter 3 for more on Communication skills.

Making an assessment

From the information you are gaining, including the cues about feelings and vulnerabilities, you will be assessing whether or not you are able to help this young person. Do you have:

- knowledge of this area of difficulty?
- expertise in this area?
- resources (including time)?

If you will not be the best source of support, are you able to refer them to another agency or support worker? If so you will need to explain this in a positive way. How to handle this effectively and sensitively is covered in Chapter 17.

If you are not able to help or refer on and they must look elsewhere for help you may need to explain this and make suggestions as to where support may be available. This may take another meeting.

If you do not have enough information, should you agree to meet again to hear more? If you are unsure about offering help, give yourself time to consider. Explain that you will need time to think about what they have told you and suggest another meeting. This will also give you time to consult your supervisor or colleagues.

If you assess that you have the knowledge, expertise and resources to offer further support then you need to make arrangements to meet again.

Contact arrangements

If a first meeting is to be followed by further contact then the place and time of meeting should be clearly agreed. Some young people find keeping appointments very difficult. Would a reminder phone call be of help?

It is also helpful for the youth worker to explain what they will do if an appointment is not kept, such as writing a note or telephoning. Some young people may need a gentle reminder that your time is precious too:

> *If you decide not to come back to see me that will be absolutely fine – but it would be helpful if you let me know so that I do not keep the time especially for you.*

As appointments sometimes need to be changed, each person should have a point of contact for the other, such as an office phone number, answerphone or place where a message can be left. The adult contacting the young person needs to check what can be said if someone else answers the phone or if others may listen to an answerphone message. This will ensure that confidentiality is not compromised. Acceptable times to phone for both parties should also be agreed.

The adult should decide whether it is wise to give their home or mobile telephone number or address. If a professional address is not available then, for client contact, a separate number with answerphone may be a better option.

Emergency contact

Depending on your role and your relationship it may be appropriate to give a young client a point of contact for emergencies. For workers who belong to an organisation, the workplace may be the point of contact. Even if that organisation has a 24 hour answering service, you may need to explain to your client how often you will receive your messages and whether, for example, you will be picking up messages over a bank holiday weekend. The youth worker must think ahead and anticipate such problems.

Giving your home or mobile telephone number could be endangering your privacy and your own peace of mind. A cry for help from a needy teenager will be difficult to respond to appropriately if it comes unexpectedly in the middle of your own domestic crisis. For the really needy the telephone number of The Samaritans or a local 24 hour service appropriate to the young person may be given in writing. You may want to hand over a small card with appropriate numbers at each meeting, for young people can lose even vital pieces of paper.

Length and frequency of contact

In formally organised relationships, such as some mentoring, a regular appointment is routinely set up with weekly or fortnightly meetings in a fixed place and for a set period of time. However, in youth work, where one-to-one encounters are more haphazard, setting a contract about how often to meet may not be feasible. One might initially agree on one meeting at a time. However, if after two or three meetings this relationship is settling into a regular routine, then a contract for a limited number of weeks should be made.

It is helpful for the young person to know that the helping relationship will have an ending. The eventual aim is for the young person to grow independent. Together you may decide on three meetings, followed by a review meeting to consider the progress made and whether you are ready to end or whether it is necessary to continue to meet for a few more sessions.

In circumstances where adolescent and youth worker see one another daily, it may be necessary to limit the formal problem-focused contact. For example during a residential weekend, in a theatre workshop or hiking through countryside one needy youngster monopolising one adult may cause problems or even danger for other participants. It is essential that the adolescent understands that the one-to-one contact should be restricted to the agreed time and place. Any attempt to break that boundary can be met with a kindly but firm:

We've agreed to meet on Tuesday at six o'clock for an hour, so we'll have plenty of time to talk about this then.

Starting and ending sessions

The suggestion above mentions starting time and intimates an ending at seven o'clock. As some young people lead very disorganised lives it is helpful to fix times for them. While some flexibility may be necessary when establishing the relationship the young person will benefit by knowing that an hour has been arranged especially for them and that to make full use of that time they will need to arrive promptly.

Ending after the allotted period can be very uncomfortable. The adult with a needy youngster can feel that talking is helping and that their young client has only just begun to open up. However, although there are occasional times when running over is necessary, having a time to end and keeping to it encourages both people to concentrate on the most important issues.

It is the responsibility of the worker to maintain the time boundaries. By mentioning the ending time some minutes ahead, the adolescent can be prepared:

We have just ten minutes until we must end today.

This may give the young person just the prompt to remember what they really meant to mention, but had not quite managed to say. However this will not stop the 'door-knob' message, when the client communicates their most important thoughts just as they are going. The worker, however curious, can acknowledge the message but it is not the moment to encourage the client to come back and talk:

That sounds important. We'll have plenty of time to think about it when we meet next.

The young person will appreciate that this is rationed time. The worker will get used to drawing sessions to a close and benefit by being able to keep their own time under control.

Talking about endings when you've only just begun!

A vulnerable young person needs to know that your relationship is for a limited time. The adolescent who is not prepared for the ending may feel rejected by you and blame it on *their own* short-comings or worthlessness. Then much of your helpful work together may be wasted. From the beginning mention the limited time and prepare for the ending. (Further discussion about how to end and how to refer can be found in Chapter 17.)

Intuitively it may seem wrong to talk about ending a relationship when you have only just got started but it is important to keep the ultimate goals in focus. Whether you are a stepping stone to further support or have responsibility for helping to maintain a change in behaviour over a particular period, your role is to help a young person through a stage of transition on their path to adulthood. The relationship will be temporary. You are only in a supporting role along part of the individual's journey to independence.

SECTION TWO: ADOLESCENTS' RELATIONSHIPS

Chapter 5

Parents

Parents have the potential to support their adolescent children and most try to do so. This chapter discusses some of the positive and negative aspects of adolescent-parent relationships. It then explores some ways in which youth workers and mentors can encourage adolescent-parent communication and a positive relationship.

Adolescents who have good relationships with their parents tend to thrive. There is substantial evidence from psychological research showing an association between good adolescent-parent relationships and good adjustment to adult life in terms of self-confidence, social competence and general psychological well being (Kenny, 1994; Rice and Mulkeen, 1995; Taylor, 1997). However, the significance of the adolescent-parent relationship can be underestimated by youth workers who mainly see young people with their peer group. While young people are observed as being influenced by friends and by peer pressure, parental influences may be less obvious. The professional helper, working from outside the family, needs to appreciate and encourage the rich potential of adolescent-parent relationships.

Adolescent-parent relationships

Nearly all adolescents have at least one parent. Studies show that even teenagers who are 'looked after' or in foster care have at least one birth parent living and most have both parents alive (Aldgate, Maluccio and Reeves, 1989). Furthermore and contrary to the perception of a distressed or rebellious young person going through a difficult time, most parents really do have their child's best interests at heart. The vast majority of parents want their children to have the best of opportunities for what they see as long term happiness and success, even if their attitudes or actions seem contrary in the short term. For some parents the circumstances of their own lives are so bad that they decide that their child will have better chances away from them, despite the high emotional cost of separation. The majority of parents aim to keep their adolescents with them and, apart from a few very inadequate parents and the few who are abusive and destructive, they try to provide circumstances that will enable their child to take on responsibilities and prepare for adulthood and independence.

Needing support at times of transition

Parents can ease the transition to adulthood with both practical help and emotional support. The issues involved in leaving home are discussed in Chapter 16 but here it is important to note that adolescents are profoundly affected by their perception of how their parents value them. Adolescents, who are viewed negatively by their parents, usually view themselves negatively and have low self-esteem. In contrast, the positive, supportive parent will show appreciation for even small successes so that the adolescent can feel good about themselves. This parent will be interested in their work, study and leisure pursuits, discussing opportunities and enabling them to weigh up situations but also allowing them to make their own decisions. The parent will also be available when things go wrong! The home can be a place of stability where the adolescent belongs and where someone cares.

The path through adolescence is marked with major changes, such as starting a new school, beginning a part-time job, going away to university, taking on a regular full-time job, embarking on or breaking up from a serious sexual relationship. Each change is followed by a period of adjustment: getting used to the loss of the familiar, taking on new responsibilities and making new relationships. It is at these stages of transition that the young person is most likely to need support and to turn to a parent. Once the adjustment has been made, parental support is no longer so crucial and the concerned parent may well be rejected...until the next time!

Sources of conflict

The relationship can be problematic because it is paradoxical. The adolescent wants to become independent of their parents but they also want their support, on and off, whilst doing so. Although there is a general understanding that adolescence is a time of 'storm and stress' research since the 1960s has shown that adolescent-parent relationships are generally stable. Evidence from a large variety of population samples suggests that, regardless of regular arguments with parents, only about one in five families are affected by major disputes and only about 'one in ten or twenty families experience a dramatic deterioration of parent-adolescent relationships' (Hill, 1993: p70). However the quality of the relationship can vary enormously. Some adolescents and parents change between periods of enjoying one another's company, blazing rows and long spells of non-communication.

Giving an overview of the research Noller (1994) reported that most arguments concentrated on everyday matters such as helping around the home, style of clothing and curfews. In contrast, areas of major difference, such as sex, drugs, politics and religion, were rarely discussed. For example there was little actual communication between parents and adolescents on sex-related matters although, when interviewed, both parents and adolescents wished for more communication.

Perhaps parents and adolescents stop communicating when they fear that talking will create a rift. They see themselves holding opposite positions where the other will be intransigent and compromise will not be an option. The lack of communication may be a strategy for maintaining the relationship. However relationships that can cope with the discussion of different points of view will ultimately be more helpful to the teenager. The young person may find that relationships can withstand differences. They will then be better prepared to make life decisions by consulting others, including their parents, and weighing up different perspectives. They will also be confident that their parents will respect their decision, whether or not they fully agree.

Parents and youth workers

Parents vary in the range of concern that they show when entrusting their adolescents into the care of youth workers. Some make extensive enquiries to ensure that an organisation has aims and policies consistent with their own beliefs, that the facilities are good and that, above all, the adults who will be taking responsibility for their child are competent and trustworthy. At the other end of the spectrum some parents consider that the youth worker provides a useful service for keeping their youngster out of their hair for a few hours at a time, or even for a whole week if a residential experience is on offer. Whatever their attitude to you and some are very supportive and a pleasure to work with, you must ensure that you treat them with respect for the benefit of the youngster in your care.

Encouraging communication

It is all too easy to perceive parents in a negative light. Sometimes their indifference to your organisation seems geared to ruining your carefully worked out programme:

> Goalkeeper Charmaine has to attend her grandmother's birthday tea on the afternoon of the most important away match of the season.
>
> Junior, lead singer in the charity show, phones to say that he has to babysit for his sister.
>
> Alexei's mother has imposed a curfew.

Occasionally a personal approach at the last minute can save the situation, but not always. Frequently the problem is due to poor communication between parent and adolescent, with each quite sure that the other was aware of the importance of the occasion and of the plans that had been unilaterally arranged. The youth worker can decrease the likelihood of such difficulties by encouraging young people to talk regularly to their parents about time commitments and about their activities in general. This in turn may open the lines of communication and extend to those more difficult to discuss areas when your programme explores topics such as drugs and sex.

While some parents take little or no interest, others seem to be constantly inter-fering. They want to know exactly what is going on and seem to give their adolescent little space for independent development. The parent unable to let go may be the first to volunteer to drive the additional mini-van. They may be the one to rally professional expertise to ensure that your entry to the local pageant will be the best in town, without understanding that the less than perfect efforts organised and executed by the youngsters themselves may be more rewarding than the 'prize for winning'.

When the scout troop needed some funds, the parents got together to organise a couple of superb fetes which raised a great deal of cash. The parents enjoyed the camaraderie and honed their organisational skills but the scouts were consigned to being 'junior helpers' and quickly lost interest. The scout leader had tactfully to reclaim the fundraising role, so that the scouts could be encouraged to raise funds by their own efforts, even though they raised less money. They would benefit by learning through first-hand experience.

It is up to the youth leader to negotiate a balance by encouraging involvement by parents when appropriate, but to tactfully limit over-involvement before it becomes oppressive.

When working with older adolescents it is often helpful to remind them to consult their parents. When living away from home they may be reluctant to admit to difficulties or failures and nor do they want to be a burden. However the parent at home might be happy to provide some emotional support and an experienced approach. Noller (1994) reviewed studies in which university students reported that their parents were the most important influences in their lives, affecting their 'future-oriented' decisions about education, careers, jobs and choice of spouse. For those who are not in regular touch with a parent it is a big step to ask for advice or even just to find out if the parent is interested. Research carried out with 16–20 year old further education students showed that those who had not adjusted well to college had poorer relationships with their parents and were receiving less emotional support than their general student population (Taylor, 1997). In interview most poorly adjusted adolescents wished that they could involve a parent in their lives but were reluctant to take a first step for fear of parental indifference or a repeat of previous rejection. Where youth worker and adolescent have the opportunity to discuss a difficult parental relationship, the adolescent might be encouraged to talk to a qualified counsellor with a view to healing rifts with parents.

Merryls' story illustrates the importance of the continuing parental rela-tionship. While a youth-worker or mentor who is not a qualified counsellor or family therapist should not attempt to unpack the emotional history of a fragile and vulnerable adolescent, they can encourage them to seek help and give them the appropriate information or referral. Recognising that problems with parents can be helped and knowing that parents as well as their children mature over time can encourage the youth worker to promote good parental relationships.

Merryl's story

17 year old Merryl was not naturally communicative. She was encouraged to meet with a counsellor because she was withdrawn and was developing an eating problem. Her brother had died from cancer when she was ten and she felt that all her problems stemmed from then. However when the counsellor asked about her parents it became clear that she did not talk to her mother and that she was very angry with her father, who had abandoned the family.

During the counselling sessions she described incidents from her childhood on a run-down estate. There had frequently been little to eat and mother had begged food and money from her own parents. This encouraged Merryl to reminisce about the 'bad times' with her mother between sessions. Merryl was eventually able to tell her life story as a coherent narrative. She was also able to acknowledge that her mother was trying to be a good parent despite their poverty.

In just eight weekly counselling sessions, Merryl moved from talking to her mother about her childhood on to their current relationship. In the last counselling session Merryl was really pleased to report that her mother had actually boasted about her to a neighbour. This was the first time she had ever believed that her mother was genuinely proud of her. She felt that with her mother's support she could succeed. From then on Merryl flourished. She started to make friends, finished her college course and then found herself a job.

Pitfall warning!

Some adolescents yearn for parental care and concern but, whatever they do, it will not be forthcoming. Do not be tempted to intervene. Leave it to the professionals. Even professional family therapists may not succeed, but they will be able to prepare the individual for disappointment and give follow-up support. This really is an area where intervention can cause more harm than good.

Working successfully with the parents

Except for circumstances where a child is being 'looked after' (in care), parents have full legal responsibility for their children. There are circumstances when it is essential for the youth worker to consult a parent about their child. Whatever the reason, preparation for the meeting or phone call is essential.

Before the contact:

- Explain to the adolescent why the contact is necessary.
- Decide what is to be discussed – and whether there are matters confidential to your relationship which should not be disclosed.

- If meeting, discuss whether or not the young person should be present.

Adapted from Wheal, 1998.

Establishing a mutually respectful relationship with the parents is vital if you are to co-operate in supporting their child. Your intervention is more likely to be received as helpful and supportive rather than offensive or undermining if you keep in mind the following:

- Before embarking on your own agenda, learn from them. Find out about their concerns and attitudes.
- The parent knows about many aspects of their child's life better than you do.
- The parent is an expert on the family history and current family situation.
- Present your ideas as suggestions rather than fully formed plans.
- Encourage their contribution and further discussion with their child.
- Include them in the planning.
- Be tactful if you realise that the parents are setting an example of hypocritical or undesirable behaviour. Remember that you are working in partnership and do not undermine them.
- Where parent and adolescent hold opposing positions, resist taking 'sides'.
- Use your negotiating skills to help them reach a solution.

Real life does not always have fairy tale endings. Sometimes the youth worker acts as mediator where parents seem to be standing in the way of a step that, to an outsider, appears clearly to be to the young person's advantage. While in fiction, such as the film Billy Elliott, a miner father can eventually accept his son's decision to train as a ballet dancer, in real life parents cannot always support plans contrary to their culture or their financial or economic situation. Sometimes the youth worker has to help the youth to come to terms with a negative decision.

Providing support

Families have their own difficulties and they may benefit from support in relation to parenting their adolescent children. Earning sufficient to feed and clothe the family, looking after an ill or elderly dependant, coping with marital breakdown or adapting to a new life in the UK may each take up much mental and physical energy. There may be little capacity remaining for concern about adolescent children, who may be deemed old enough to look after themselves. One of the tasks of parenting is to set boundaries and provide examples of desirable behaviour until the young adult has developed sufficient internal strength to decide on and adhere to their own boundaries and to behave responsibly within society. However, when confronted by a powerful adolescent who seems to know all the answers, it is easier for some parents to let them go their own way and to abdicate responsibility. Other parents are so fearful of losing control that they exercise an authoritarian style of parenting. The adolescent might respond in the short term with outward conformity and obedience but in the long run the authoritarian approach frequently leads to rebellion, to adolescents leaving home and to relationships with parents breaking down (Noller, 1994).

Those professionals who have experience in helping young people through this process can support parents and adolescents by encouraging them to discuss their difficulties, their feelings and their options. By communicating openly they may be able to understand each other's perspectives and reach some solutions. Parents need to learn flexibility and how to cope with change. Adolescents learn that life is not fair and that some obstacles are non-negotiable. They will both benefit from learning that their relationship is valuable because a warm and positive relationship with parents is strongly associated with successful adjustment to life as a young adult.

Parents with problems

The beginning of this chapter mentioned that some parents are unable to care adequately for their children. Parents may be abusive or neglectful or both. Those who neglect their children may do so because they themselves have a mental illness or because they are abusing drugs or alcohol. If health visitors, schools, social services and child protection agencies are vigilant, then children and adolescents at risk of harm will be on a Child Protection Register and should be receiving support. However, some families are good at hiding their problems and evading 'outside interference'. Adolescents, like children, can suffer in silence, believing that their present position is better than it would be if they told of their predicament. Occasionally a trusted youth worker or mentor may gradually come to realise that the withdrawn young person with whom they are working, has a secret home life.

Supporting a young person from a family with severe problems may be very hard work. As in the case of John on page 46, trust may be very difficult to establish and just as hard to maintain. The young person may never before have experienced a stable and mutually trusting relationship. In this case there were no child protection issues to consider as John was almost an adult in the eyes of the law and there were no younger children at home. If he had been younger or had younger siblings then Asma would have needed to follow the child protection procedures.

Children and adolescents who come from homes where there is physical or sexual abuse, neglect, an alcoholic parent or domestic violence all miss out on the harmonious and supportive family environment which provide the optimal conditions for their development. In addition to the trauma suffered by the young person, such families usually communicate poorly and have low tolerance of one another's behaviours. Geldard and Geldard (1999) conclude that 'the adolescent may be subjected to levels of stress and anxiety which will make adaptive progression to adulthood more difficult' (p26). Where there is already social services involvement the role of the youth worker or mentor is to provide relaxed support just to encourage the young person to take up professional therapeutic help. In these cases intervention should be left to the professionals.

John's secret home life

John's clothes always looked a bit rumpled and he appeared to be a rather serious and somewhat depressed 17 year old, but he attended his remedial lessons punctually. His support worker Asma was pleased with his progress because when he was with her he made great strides, though his homework was messy and usually incomplete. He responded to her praise.

Over a term he began to talk a little about himself. He was the youngest of five children and the only one still at home. The others had 'got out' and he was left with his mother. Over many weeks the stories of a chaotic home life emerged. Friends had never been taken home from school. Although the older two boys had done reasonably well at school and were both independent and working, the others were faring less well. Eventually Asma began to realise that John's mother was an alcoholic. Her problem had been growing increasingly worse over the past few years but the children had coped and never told anyone. Now John was coping with her alone – but not coping with himself.

Asma consulted her colleagues and her supervisor. She was not equipped to give the sort of support that John really needed and he was too old for the local social services. However the local youth counselling service were happy to accept a referral. She explained to John that she could continue to support him with his work but that he might find counselling support helpful. She also told him about Al-ateen.

He was reluctant to do anything for many months and during that time Asma did a great deal of listening alongside the academic support work. Other problems emerged. Asma surprised herself as she managed to control her reactions while John expressed his anger, became erratic in his attendance and then returned for help. Their sessions ended with the academic year. Some time later Asma heard that John was attending a youth counselling service.

Further reading

Wheal, A. (1998) Working with Parents. In *Adolescence: Positive Approaches for Working with Young People.* Lyme Regis: Russell House Publishing.

Chapter 6

Changing Family Relationships: Separation, Divorce and Re-marriage

This chapter focuses on the difficulties faced by young people when there are major family changes such as parental separation, divorce or remarriage. Based on recent research from the fields of psychology and psychotherapy, ways of supporting young people are suggested.

Family differences

All families are different. Some teenagers have parents in their late twenties and early thirties while others have parents in their fifties or sixties. Many young people live with their biological parents who are married to one another, but many do not. Many will be living with a single parent, usually, but not always, their mother. For some a parent will have died through accident or illness when they were young. Some may never have known their fathers, while others may remember a time when their parents were together. A young person may be living with an adoptive or foster family for a variety of reasons.

In the UK one in four children under the age of 16 will have experienced divorce (Rodgers and Pryor, 1998). Some will have contact with their non-resident parent but others will not. Some are content and comfortable with their family, while others are unhappy or embarrassed and would prefer other people not to know about their family situation.

For many adolescents an untraditional family shape provides all the love, support and stability which they require for growth and contentment. However others remember better times. Ideally, they would like to return to the situation when they were living together with both parents. For the discontented young person, family members may not provide the support that they need in times of transition and stress.

Separation and divorce

Understanding the range of very different experiences and the ongoing disruption that can accompany separation and divorce can help the youth worker to support a young person going through dramatic family change.

Divorce is not a one-off event. Dowling and Gorell Barnes (2000) describe how children and adolescents become involved in what can be a protracted process as the relationship between parents deteriorates. The process, which involves loss for the adolescent and the need to grieve and adapt to new circumstances, continues after the decision to separate or divorce, after the legal process and after one parent leaves home. Frequently the children are emotionally involved. They may feel guilty themselves and responsible for their parents' predicament and they may desperately want to mend the marriage. Others may want to escape from the unhappy environment.

Practical solutions to parental economic problems also have emotional effects on the children. After divorce some have to move out of the family home which may mean moving schools and losing long-term friends from neighbourhoods and youth organisations. Starting again at school and making new friends is difficult at any age, but particularly when life at home is unsettled. The freshly separated parent who is struggling with being alone and facing social or economic difficulties may not have the time or the emotional strength to be as available and supportive as previously. Teenage children are particularly affected if a parent is depressed and the parenting skills deteriorate.

Even these upsetting changes may only be a beginning. Within two years after a divorce one or both parents may have found a new partner. The adolescent may feel hostile to the new intruder out of loyalty to the other parent. Or they may feel angry or anxious that the new partner will take away some of the attention and care that they have been accustomed to receive. Alternatively they may see the intruder as taking over 'their' job of caring for their mother. Sometimes parents are so wrapped up in their new relationship that they do not consider the needs of their adolescent child. They may also consider them to be old enough to be independent of them and not really recognise the need for ongoing support.

If marriage ensues then the young person may have to get used to another whole new family. Step-siblings may be ideal companions but they may also be competitors. If a new baby arrives the older sibling is often expected to welcome the new brother or sister and help out with the additional chores and babysitting. The adolescent may feel put upon or neglected. A step-parent may also have different parenting values and a young person can get confused with changes and pressures to conform to new house rules.

Sometimes there are two new households but the teenager feels that they are not really wanted in either. Feeling rejected they may act out their own feelings of distress and unworthiness. Living with the reshaped family may be so uncomfortable that they may try to leave home before they are emotionally or economically ready.

Many children feel that they are to blame for the break up of the marriage. If only they had behaved better, their parents would not have argued about them. Another child might blame just one parent, without being able to see that both parents had responsibility for the marriage and their relationship. If all the conflict has been conducted quietly, then the separation might come as a terrible shock. Whatever the circumstances the teenager may feel unable to express their own feelings of loss for fear of 'upsetting' the parents and making matters worse. While some 'act out' or behave badly, many more are unable to concentrate at school, to socialise normally, to eat or to sleep. Some self-harm by cutting themselves or dull the pain by using drugs.

Risk factors

With so many life-changing circumstances to adjust to, it is not surprising that children from families who have experienced separation and divorce are at greater risk of doing less well than children from intact families. Dowling and Gorell Barnes (2000) report that such children are more likely to:

- Perform less well at school, gaining fewer academic qualifications.
- Have increased behavioural problems.
- Need to see a GP or have a stay in hospital.
- Report more depressive symptoms.
- Become sexually active at a younger age.
- Become a parent earlier.

However they stress that not all children from such families experience these problems. Where there is still security, attachment and support for the child as an individual, they will develop an emotional understanding that, although their parents have separated, each of them continues to love them and continues to be actively involved in parenting them. Then many of the problems can be mitigated.

Youth worker support

Support from outside the family may help a young person to adjust to new situations too. The youth worker can provide space and a safe haven where the youngster can be themselves. They may want to talk about how life has changed from before the time of separation up to the present time. They may want to express their present feelings and discuss the losses that they have experienced. Talking with an understanding outsider may be the only opportunity to talk selfishly about what they have lost and to express their anger safely, without causing more family distress.

Steer away from the rights and wrongs of the parental relationship and to try to focus on their own difficulties. Allow as long as they need to grieve and then suggest thinking about present problems. Can some of these be tackled?

Many children voice the hope of reconciliation and the dream that their parents will get back together again. Colluding with this hope is unlikely to help. If the parents have made their decision and acted on it, then the child needs to learn to accept the new reality. Help them to think about the new individual relationships that they have with each parent and from whom they will ask for support in times of transition or when things go wrong. They may need to work out an acceptable way of voicing their own concerns, if not to both parents, then at least to one. If communication has broken down then it needs to be re-established. Only then will they be able to move forward with confidence on their own.

Case study: Karen's repeated failures

Karen was an able student but she kept failing her GCSEs. Although her coursework was very good, she failed to attend her exams and twice she vomited in the exam room. Her youth worker heard her woes and then realised that Karen's reactions were much the same in other testing situations. She excelled in kick-boxing and was easily the best girl in the club, but she was always ill on the day of the competitions with outside clubs, and never managed to take part.

Although she seemed fed up, Karen was willing to talk. She lived with her mother, two brothers and a sister and she had a regular boyfriend who was in his early twenties. The youth worker noticed that she never mentioned her father. She wondered aloud whether Karen would be willing to say anything about him, although she would understand if not. Karen said that she really did not want to talk about him at all but then she changed her mind and the family story came tumbling out.

Karen was the eldest and she had been the apple of her father's eye. She had been bright at primary school and a promising athlete. He had encouraged her at school and later enrolled her at a junior athletics club where she had excelled in local competitions. He had always been there to support her.

When she was about eleven, her father and mother began to quarrel openly and violently at home. Sometimes Karen intervened and once she was injured in a fight and a social worker became involved. A year or two later father left home. Mother had never forgiven him and nor had Karen. She would not talk to him or about him. However he lived nearby and he regularly kept in touch with his other children. If Karen happened to pick up the phone when he rang, she would pass over the receiver to another family member without saying a word.

The story came out in such a flood that the youth worker realised that this was significant. Karen had never spoken about this before. The youth worker again wondered whether it would be helpful to talk to a counsellor. The usually bolshy Karen agreed to think about it. She was surprised that talking about her father had been possible at all. A few days later she inquired about the counsellor.

In six focused sessions the counsellor helped Karen to make sense of her history. Her past successes had been very much bound up with her father and her desire to please him. She talked a great deal about her childhood. When her father was not around to support her, she started to fail. She was very angry with him. She was not even going to give him the satisfaction of hearing her voice. However she could grudgingly admit that the other children saw him regularly and that they seemed happy to go out with him. Nevertheless she wanted nothing to do with him.

One evening, on picking up the phone and hearing his voice she found herself responding. She was very surprised at herself and at what she heard. It seemed he was still interested in her, however much she was blocking him out of her life. Slowly they resumed contact. Their conversations were awkward but Karen found herself growing in confidence. This extended to other areas of her life. She began

> to talk to class mates at college, where before she had been reluctant to relate to anyone. She started to socialise and to believe in herself again. With help from the college she was able to take her examinations and this time she passed.
>
> Eighteen months later she dropped in to see the youth worker. She came to show off her new baby but also to say that she was settled. Supported by her boyfriend and her mother she would be studying for further qualifications so that she could get a reasonable job and help support her family.

Karen was blocking her own success but she was quite unable to locate the source of her distress. Her broken relationship with her father was so upsetting that she could never allow herself to think about it. The encounter with the youth worker provided a safe enough situation to talk about her family. The youth worker had been sensitive enough to recognise that counselling could be helpful but she had not pushed Karen at all. Karen had chosen to meet the counsellor when she felt ready.

Divorce as a loss

Like death, parental divorce can be an emotional experience which triggers grief and mourning in the adolescent. Just as in bereavement (see Chapter 15) they may go through the same phases: shock and denial, anger and/or guilt, yearning for the old status quo, pining for the absent parent, feeling confused, depressed and unable to concentrate and, perhaps, fear of new relationships (Raphael, 1994). Support from an understanding outsider may be very welcome.

Useful websites

Parentline plus for parents, professionals and young people and children: http://www.parentlineplus.org.uk/data/children/index.html

'When parents begin new relationships': http://www3.extension.umn.edu/parentsforever/unit6/unit6-6c.asp

Chapter 7

Cultural Identities

This chapter focuses on working with individuals from different cultural backgrounds. It provides definitions for 'ethnicity' and 'racism' and describes a model of identity development for individuals living in ethnic minority groups. Ways of working with individuals and groups are suggested.

In an increasingly multi-cultural world, youth workers are likely to meet young people from diverse cultures. Some London Boroughs have school pupils from over one hundred different cultures. While some adolescents have arrived from overseas, others are the children of first, or second generation immigrants or belong to minority groups who have been in the UK over hundreds of years. Their values and expectations, or that of their families, may differ from those of the majority community, particularly on issues concerning social behaviour, sexual relationships and marriage, and educational and career choices. These areas of conflict have to be faced by the young person already coping with the usual challenges of adolescence. To support a young person from a culture different from their own, the youth worker needs to be able to recognise and understand the differences. Before embarking on cross-cultural work we each need to understand our own individual cultural identity.

Values, assumptions and prejudices

Recognition of our own attitudes, assumptions and prejudices, as discussed in Chapter 3, is vital preparation before initiating helpful relationships with young people from other cultures. This applies to helpers from minority and majority cultures alike. Sue et al. (1998) advise that to work effectively we each need to be aware of our own cultural heritage and to have thought about the history of our own family in relation to our local community and the wider community.

We each need to consider how discrimination and stereotyping affect us individually and also how we use power that we derive from our own community affiliations.

Racism and ethnic groups

Racism tends to exist in most situations where people from different cultures live and work together. In many communities and institutions the leaders would deny the existence of racism because they believe they have countered it successfully.

Self evaluation exercise

Have I experienced being an outsider? Was this because of the colour of my skin, my accent, my dress or my behaviour? How did I feel and how did I react? Is this an ongoing experience for me? How does it affect my relationships with a) individuals from the majority group and b) individuals from minority groups very different from my own?

For a white youth worker living and working in a white majority community: Have I considered how I may have benefited from being a member of the majority? Do I have an inner feeling of superiority? Do I draw my confidence, or power, from being part of the majority? How does this affect my relationships with those outside the majority group?

However, it tends to remain influential, if hidden. Chris Gaine (1995) showed that even in primary schools where children appeared to their teachers to be working and playing amicably and respectfully together, hidden tape recorders picked up racist remarks.

Gaine provides some useful definitions:

> An **ethnic group** is a group of people who share a history, key cultural features, such as religion and language and a range of less definable customs perhaps associated with birth, marriage, food and the like. It may be that they are distinguished by some physical features (hair, eye or skin colour, height, facial features) but this may not be universal or excluding.
>
> Gaine, 1995: p25.

> **Ethnicity** is about how people define themselves off from others. In this sense Jews are an ethnic group, Punjabi Sikhs are an ethnic group British Poles are an ethnic group and, loosely speaking, so are the Welsh.
>
> Gaine, 1995: p25.

Gaine also suggests that whilst ethnicity is a mode of being, racism is a mode of oppression:

> ...**Racism** is a belief in the superiority of one group over others. The 'others' are currently defined by a confused mixture of essentialist qualities rooted in biology or culture, or a confused amalgam of colour, culture, language or religion.
>
> Gaine, 1995: p28.

Young people are easy prey to racism. It is easier to project one's anxieties about inadequacy onto other people and to make jokes at the expense of minority ethnic groups. An individual may gain relief from their own anxiety about feeling stupid, ugly or alone, by sharing a joke at the expense of a minority to become part of an 'in-crowd'. Luxmoore (2000) relates his experience as a youth worker being welcomed by a new group of youngsters with:

… jokes about black people, gay people, Asian people, Irish people, women. They watched me. If I laughed I was implicated. If I remained stony-faced I was a killjoy.

Luxmoore, 2000: p89.

An inexperienced youth worker, anxious to establish relationships, could have been sucked in to condoning racist or sexist comments. Luxmoore recognised that the young people were anxious about him, an outsider, taking over their project and that they wanted to see whether he would be 'one of them' or on their side. Outright disapproval of their jokes before establishing the relationship would have been pointless. Instead he had to demonstrate a lack of interest in the subject of their jokes, indicating that he would not join in, but that at the same time he was not rejecting them and their feelings of uncertainty and insecurity. As Luxmoore began to work with the group over a few weeks he was able to show them the difference between laughing *at* others and laughing *with* others.

Instances of racism, sexism or other offensive behaviour should always be challenged. A well-established and trusted youth worker should also explain why 'jokes', nick-names and some gesturing is in fact offensive, damaging and unacceptable.

Specific interventions should be well considered. Brief interventions which aim to 'teach' young people about prejudice or racism may do more harm than good (Gaine, 1995). Where there are individuals from different ethnic groups among the white majority, they may feel particularly exposed and may be discomforted by even more 'jokey' behaviour from their equally uncomfortable classmates. However longer term interventions are likely to be more effective. For example inviting an adult from a different culture to take part in a programme over a few weeks allows the young people to get to know and respect the adult. Then firmly held beliefs, prejudices and stereotyping behaviour can be challenged.

Understanding different perspectives

For those preparing to work in an area where many young people come from a particular ethnic group, it is helpful to learn about their cultural history and experiences. Key areas would include:

- **Cultural heritage**: including spiritual or religious beliefs and typical family hierarchical structure.
- **Historical background**: such as why, when and how their families came to live in the present community.
- **Life experiences**: including typical difficulties encountered at school or work.
- **Family expectations**: including pressures affecting educational and career choices and marriage and future lifestyle.

The more the youth worker understands about the family and community pressures, the easier it is to place in context some of the concerns brought by individuals. For example a talented young artist or athlete may not be receiving much encouragement from parents whose cultural perspective is to see art or sport as time-wasting distractions from the ideal of gaining professional qualifications in law or medicine. The confused and dissatisfied young person may be at the heart of a culture clash where teachers and parents are both encouraging their development – but in different directions.

In some cultures regard and respect for what is best for the whole family must take precedence over the opportunities for advancement for any individual family member:

> *A highly intelligent and hard-working schoolgirl was leaving school at 16 to work in the family restaurant. She could have passed her A levels and gained a place at a good university, but her father was not interested in her education and he needed her immediate help. While teachers and a youth worker argued fervently on her behalf, the girl reacted quite calmly and accepted her father's authority. No-one knew whether she eventually found an opportunity to return to education.*

Getting involved

While a youth worker may broaden their perspectives by working with young people from a different ethnic group, getting involved as an equal participant in the community rather than being an outside 'expert' may be an even more effective way of learning. Community events or celebrations can provide the opportunity to meet ethnic minority members on a more equal footing than one's professional role. Whether moving furniture or making food there will be the chance to learn through observation and communication. The more the youth worker understands about a culture, the more easily they will be able to stand beside the young person and understand their world view.

Acquiring this level of cultural understanding will only be possible where there is one large fairly homogeneous ethnic minority group, (and almost all community groups turn out to be full of individual differences on getting to know them!). In areas with peoples from many different minority groups the youth worker can only get to know the important cultural characteristics of each group slowly. In such circumstances the youth worker will have to learn by talking with individuals and discussing cultural similarities and differences.

Identity development for adolescents from ethnic minority groups

'Identity crisis', a phrase frequently used to express adolescent difficulties, can be an apt description for the confusion faced by an adolescent from an ethnic minority background trying to find their place in 21st century UK culture (a culture which is almost impossible to define). The process of cultural identity development is described below because it can give some clues about different adolescent attitudes and behaviours and the difficulties faced at different stages of development.

Research has shown that the process of identity development is much the same for young people from a variety of minority groups growing up within a different majority. Sue et al. (1998) have developed a 'Minority Identity Development Model' (MID) describing the stages of the process, starting in childhood.

Stage 1: Conformity
The minority individual (child or new immigrant) prefers the dominant majority group's cultural values and norms. For example: they may idealise the celebration of Christmas with tree, turkey and presents and denigrate their own culture's low-key winter festival. They consider themseves members of the majority culture and try to conform and behave accordingly.

Stage 2: Dissonance
Slowly the child breaks down the denial and begins to accept that they are 'different'. They become aware of the positive aspects and strengths of their own minority group. At the same time they will feel ashamed and embarrassed about their previously held 'conformity' attitudes.

Stage 3: Resistance and immersion
The individual (perhaps, by now, the young adolescent) begins to appreciate and endorse only their own minority group's strengths. They may frequently and vehemently reject white middle-class cultural norms. For example, if they are from a group with a traditional religion they may now regularly attend the place of worship, temple, synagogue or mosque and adhere strictly to all the traditional rules, perhaps with greater intensity than their parents.

Stage 4: Introspection
The developing adolescent begins to question their own rigidly held cultural practices. They increasingly turn their attention to themselves as individuals and to their own autonomy.

Stage 5: Synergetic articulation and awareness
The individual (perhaps in late adolescence) eventually begins to find a psychologically healthy balance between their belonging to their own minority group and their comfortable participation in the wider majority culture. They feel self-fulfilment in regard to their own minority cultural identity and increasingly self-confident about all their cross-cultural relationships in the adult world. They may develop a positive non-denigratory way of relating to people from other minority cultures. (The latter is significant because youths from one minority group often fight turf wars or scapegoat youngsters from other minority groups.)

It may be a very great challenge for a young person to engage in stages 4 and 5 when they are still living in the parental home. Sadly not all individuals reach stage 5, just as some adults never achieve full independence and maturity. However it will help a youth worker relating to a young person to consider the stage that they may have reached. To do this, observe their behaviour and attitudes towards:

- members of the majority culture
- members of their own culture
- members of other minority cultures
- themselves

(Adapted from Sue et al., 1998)

Establishing a cultural identity is not easy. The Chinese boy may find:

- He is too Chinese for his white college friends.
- He is too English for his parents.
- He is too old-fashioned for his Chinese friends.

Unfortunately even achieving a maturely balanced cultural identity might not help in coping with differences of opinion regarding culture in one's own family.

Conflicting loyalties: family versus the outside world

'My parents don't understand me' is a common adolescent lament and is apt for the young person trying to straddle two conflicting cultures. Some individuals cross back and forth across the threshold of two different worlds every day. Difficulty is commonly experienced by girls, for example from families originating in India or Pakistan who see themselves as the same as their white and black school friends until they reach puberty. Soon after that and certainly by the age of 15 or 16 they find that their social freedom is curtailed by parents and brothers, who want to protect their honour and the family's good name. While their counterparts are allowed to go out in the evening and to have boyfriends some British Asian girls have six o'clock curfews and they have to hide any relationships with boys. While individuals whose behaviour is at stage 3 of cultural identity development have no difficulty keeping to the family rules, those at stage 4 may want to kick the boundaries. For the most mature at stage 5 their reaction to family expectations will depend on the type of balance they have found: some will be patient and bide their time while others will rebel.

While, like Sunita in the case study on page 58, some young people can manage compromise and find appropriate outlets for their feelings (talking to their friends, rebelling in small but not harmful ways) others may grow increasingly unhappy and turn in on themselves. When cultural conflict leads to an impasse a girl may consider herself to be in an intolerable situation with feelings of depression, hopelessness or despair. At this stage she may even consider suicide as the only escape. Research has shown that young women in the UK whose families originate from the Indian sub-continent are at greater risk of committing suicide or attempting suicide than their peers (The Samaritans, cited in Donnellan, 2000).

If a young person makes any mention of suicide, take it seriously (see Chapter 14).

Real fear of abduction abroad for an arranged marriage or any similar situation should also be taken seriously. Advice for black and Asian women is available from: Southall Black Sisters 020 8571 9595.

Interventions

Establishing a cross-cultural relationship requires all the usual key qualities and sensitivities together with awareness of the following:

Case study: Sunita

Sunita loved drama lessons and always took part in school plays. In her final year at school she rehearsed diligently in her key role and then discovered that the performance was to take place on three consecutive evenings. The family rule (and her community's custom) was that she needed to be home by six o'clock. (If she was delayed by a class detention she embarrassingly had to get a note from the teacher to show to her father.) Father flatly refused his permission for evening performances and he also objected to her costume, which did not conform to modesty requirements.

Her teacher was cross that Sunita had not anticipated the problem. The teacher was more concerned about the production than about Sunita's predicament.

The youth worker from the Asian mothers and daughters group tried to arrange a compromise whereby Sunita's mother would accompany her each evening and escort her home. However Sunita decided that the embarrassment of wearing a modified costume, unlike the rest of the cast, leaving with her mother each evening and missing the final night party were all too much to endure. She decided that pulling out and coping with the wrath of her teacher and the non-understanding of her fellow cast-members would be an easier option than going against her father's wishes.

- In some cultures counselling or talking of private or family matters outside the family would be totally inappropriate. It might be considered shameful or a sign of weakness.
- Assurance regarding confidentiality would need to be carefully spelled out. (Some young people particularly choose a youth worker or counsellor from another culture because they are very unlikely to have contact with their family or community. This is their safeguard for confidentiality.)
- Resistance to 'rapport' may be culturally based rather than a personal inability to share or trust.
- In some cultures problems take somatic form e.g. in ailments such as headaches or stomach upsets.

Process for individual work

1. Start by focusing on any problem which the young person has mentioned. Take time and encourage the young person to describe the difficulties in detail. Initially they may expect a practical solution – but for the time being you are just establishing the relationship.
2. Focus on the problem, rather than on them as a person, which may be too intrusive.
   e.g. Respond: 'That is a difficult situation to be in' rather than 'You seem to be in a difficult situation'.
3. Reframe a problem so the young person can see some achievable goals.
4. Use a one step at a time approach to working out how to attain a particular goal. As well as providing practical help, this will help to reduce embarrassment or shame.

5. Normalise the problem by explaining that other people their age have these sorts of problems. You can show that you understand the particular difficulties of cultural adjustment, and conflicting family values.
6. If focusing on solutions check whether the young person will need to consult others. Remember that they may be too polite to say that your 'straightforward' solution is totally unacceptable. Check out feasibility at each stage.

(Adapted from Sue, 1999)

Referrals to 'mother tongue' counselling or same culture support.

Some young people prefer to talk in their mother tongue, especially those who cannot yet express themselves well in English, and others just prefer to be supported by a person who shares their cultural background. In some parts of the UK 'mother tongue' counselling services are available for members of some ethnic minority groups. Some social services also provide interpretation services. See Chapter 17 for making referrals.

Group work

For some young people joining a group of similar background is more helpful than getting individual support. Indeed their difficulties may be due to isolation and lack of community. For example some young refugees and asylum seekers find themselves in hostels, with no money, having to adjust to new climate and culture and they feel lonely and get increasingly depressed. Others may live with a family member but have the burden of being spokesperson and negotiator for the family with no opportunity of developing their own talents or even having a social life. Norton (2001) quotes a youth worker explaining that refugees from war-torn Somalia may not want to talk about the traumas they have been through too early. What they need are the facilities where they can meet together and enjoy themselves like any other group of young people. Where refugee community organisations have been established they may be able to provide refugee leaders to offer advice and support and to lead some activities.

In the USA group programmes have been run successfully for black male youths by black mentors (Leonard et al., 1999). In training each mentor is encouraged to consider their own role as black person in society, in work and at home, and to think about their own role models and heroes. They examine their feelings about their sense of purpose and satisfaction as a black person and also what makes them fearful and angry. The mentors discuss how they see black youth today and the opportunities and dangers that they face, including issues of low self-esteem and the concerns of drugs and violence. In group work the black male youths learn about their culture and their responsibilities. Guided by their mentor/role models, they begin to take pride in themselves. The groups also help them to raise their aspirations and to see the value of education.

Further reading

Norton, R. and Cohen, B. (2000) *Out of Exile: Developing Youth Work With Young Refugees.* Youth Work Press.

Chapter 8

Peer Relationships: Positive Development and Negative Influences

This chapter begins by examining adolescent social groups and how friendships within them support social and emotional development. However social groups can be exclusive and rejecting. Some individuals who are unable to join 'normal' social groups may be drawn towards the anti-social 'gang' or the deviant peer group. The indications for youth worker intervention and support are discussed.

By early adolescence almost all individuals share an understanding of the social rules which govern their interactions with other young people. Behaviour patterns, evolving through primary school, result in peer culture whereby children follow social codes and procedures (Youniss, McLellan and Strouse, 1994). Children's peer group rules may not always be spoken but are widely accepted. Examples of peer group rules may include:

- One does not 'snitch' or 'tell on a friend'.
- A bigger or older child has more power and may expect deference.
- Someone giving something expects to receive something equally valuable in return.

In the early years peer interaction takes place under the watchful eye of a parent or teacher who can intervene when necessary. By early adolescence the adult supervision has receded although some individuals might need or even welcome adult support or intervention.

Adolescent peer groups

Between the ages of 10 and 13 most individuals have to negotiate the big move from primary school into secondary school. In addition to adjusting to new teachers, new buildings, new rules and harder work, there are also many new peers to meet. How to 'fit in' is a great concern. Meeting for the first time, young people may start categorising those individuals who seem to have desirable attributes and similar interests: these are the peers with whom they wish to be friends. They apply the learned social rules and respond positively to one another as they develop potential friendships. Gradually these individuals coalesce into groups.

The peer groups or 'crowds' that they join, or fail to join, are social systems where individuals share interests, attitudes and often abilities and personal characteristics too (Brown, Mory and Kinney, 1994). Individuals may express their crowd membership by the way they behave and dress and they may have a particular territory where they hang out such as a playground area or a street corner. Different groups have different foci (with matching credentials) such as the popular crowd (good-looking, outgoing), the sporty crowd (good at sport), the studious crowd (academically bright), the 'nerds' (aeroplane spotters or stamp collectors) and the middle of the road 'normals' (neither outstanding nor 'weird'). Each crowd has a particular image, of which insiders and outsiders are aware, and the individual members draw their social identity from that membership (Youniss et al., 1994). Some individuals see themselves as belonging to more than one group to satisfy diverse interests and different aspects of their personalities. They will spend time with friends in each crowd. They perceive themselves as having a broader identity than just the one group can provide and are perhaps trying to forge their own separate identity.

The adolescent crowd may also be a source of emotional support. As the young person becomes increasingly independent of their parents so their crowd of particular friends can become a 'second family' (Muisener, 1994). If things go wrong, and they feel angry, unhappy, uncomfortable, rejected or aggrieved they are increasingly likely to turn to these peers for support. Girls are particularly good at providing emotional support and care. However, where group members are competitive and vying for their own status and for individual goals, their relationships may be more superficial and less supportive. These social experiences within groups all contribute to the overall psychological development of the individual.

The 'loner' and the 'misfit'

Those who do not fit in to the available crowds may experience problems. Some of these outsiders may take pride in their individuality, style themselves as 'nonconformists' or 'eccentrics' and cope tolerably well. An example would be the 'swat', the intellectually able student in a non-academic school, who has to withstand the taunts of their peers so that they can pass the required exams and eventually meet others sharing their academic interests. Without true friendship they may rely on support from family or other interested adults.

Other youngsters identify themselves as outsiders or 'loners'. Loner is a social category recognised by most adolescents, even though it is not an observable group (Youniss, McLellan and Strouse, 1994). The loner may feel rejected. They may acknowledge the characteristics required to belong to the group they wish to join but deny their lack of them. They may also lack social skills. If they feel stigmatised as an outcast and yearn company they may join other 'misfits' for companionship. The rejected child frequently finds other rejected children as these are the only friends available (Dishion, 1990). Together they may start to dabble in anti-social behaviour and so evolve into a deviant peer group (see below).

Exclusive groups

Why are some rejected? Most youth workers will have met young individuals, not natural 'loners', desperate to join a particular group by whom they are ignored or shunned. An individual may go to great lengths to bribe or inveigle a way in but never really be accepted. Brown et al. (1994) suggest that members of a popular 'in' crowd may have many friendship overtures from outsiders wanting to join the group. The 'popular' girl may reject the overture if she perceives the potential friend as not matching up to the group image. (Infiltration by the non good-looking may dilute the desirability of the group.) From those wishing to join, crowd members (unconsciously) select only those who fit their redefined profile. So the group becomes an exclusive 'clique', impermeable to outsiders. Outside interference from a youth worker on behalf of the 'outsider' is unlikely to have any long-term effect of real acceptance. Instead the 'outsider' may do better to pursue new interests where they can meet a new, more open crowd and stand a higher chance of acceptance.

Exclusivity is also a feature of social crowds where members all belong to a particular ethnic group. Brown, Mory and Kinney (1994) suggest that in multi-ethnic schools, ethnic group-based crowds form early in adolescence and then the image and identity of the group is increasingly defined by the racial and cultural differences between crowd members and 'others'. There are pressures to declare the best of one's own ethnic heritage; there are sanctions against acting like or adopting the customs of those from other groups. The youth worker hoping to promote inter-racial friendships may set up activities where the individuals from different groups will meet and co-operate. However there are also outside pressures to maintain the exclusivity of these groups. Many parents and religious leaders from, for example Black, Moslem, or Jewish communities, hope that their adolescents will marry partners from their own faith or racial background. Since marriage partners often develop from friendships forged within youth groups there is pressure to maintain exclusivity. Indeed some youth movements are founded primarily to promote that and the youth leader is similarly committed. Hence the outsider may be welcome as a visiting onlooker but not as a participant.

Romantic relationships

By middle adolescence individuals may have some true friendships with members of their own sex but, with sexual maturity and romantic intentions, they need to learn about relating to members of the opposite sex. Furman and Wehner (1994) suggest how dating skills develop. Some adolescents have little experience in relating to members of the opposite sex and will only feel comfortable if making or receiving an approach whilst in a crowd. Building on these experiences they will develop the social skills required for casual dating. They will learn how to demonstrate friendship, caregiving and support. They may also, depending on their cultural norms and maturity, experiment with sex. From here a pairing may develop into a stable and exclusive long-term relationship. (Although heterosexual relationships are the focus here, the development of homosexual relationships is similar. See Chapter 12.)

Requests for help with romantic relationships

Occasionally an adolescent will seek help from their youth worker or mentor when faced with boyfriend or girlfriend difficulties. **Be cautious: this may require professional relationship counselling. Relationship issues are often tied into identity development.** (Raskin and Waterman, 1994).

> *Amina is in a relationship that is not going according to her preconceived plan. She wants to tell her parents but, if she does so, Rav will be obliged (by community pressure) to marry her. He wants his space and independence. She is already feeling guilty.*

> *16 year old Dave believes he has found the perfect partner in Jana and wants to get engaged now. She is not ready to make such a commitment but wants to remain as his girlfriend. His real difficulty is about contemplating an uncertain and insecure future…*

The adolescent may be in a state of confusion about why they want to continue the relationship. The attachment may have raised uncomfortable issues and they may be ready to find out more about themselves. The amateur counsellor/advice-giver may help a couple to look at possible options in the immediate situation but is unlikely to have the skills to help the individuals recognise and understand their real feelings. The more helpful response would be to listen and be supportive but to explain that the local youth counsellor will also take them seriously and be better able to discuss the situation.

Pitfalls

The isolated individual who has difficulty with all relationships may approach for help 'with meeting the right person'. Whilst you are providing ample opportunity to discuss problems, they might develop a crush on you (Raskin and Waterman, 1994). Safeguard your own professional position by referring on this young person for professional help. Do not ignore the plea for support because difficulties could be the result of family dysfunction, abuse or neglect and if so therapy would be valuable.

The value of the peer group

So far this chapter has discussed how peer relationships support the adolescent in various ways. To summarise they may provide security in an unfamiliar environment, be a source of emotional support, give shape to social identity and provide a launching pad from which to meet others and learn about romantic relationships. Peer groups are not static for they may change membership and alter focus as the members mature. However, for the individual, peers will help to form the ideas and opinions of later adolescence and so possibly influence leisure activities, interests, politics, religious beliefs and career choice.

Making good friends...and then losing touch

For a young person forced to move away from a crowd of good friends the loss is great. Reasons for moving may be beyond a young person's control, such as the family breadwinner changing jobs, or parents separating, or emigration to escape from war or persecution. The easiest time to move is when an adolescent's age-group is going through a time of transition (such as moving to secondary school or post-GCSE move to sixth form or further education college). Then new peer groups are forming and established ones re-forming and the new face may be more readily accepted into the crowd. But where crowds are already established only the individuals with the most obvious group image credentials (sporting prowess, stunning good looks or a matching group history) will find ready acceptance in the more cliquey groups. For most it will take time to form new friendships and for many these will not feel as close and meaningful as those left behind.

Individuals moving into an area may value some discreet support from a youth worker who can indicate the crowd who are most likely to be welcoming. In some circumstances the youth worker needs to be particularly aware of the additional difficulties that a newcomer may be experiencing.

Immigrants, refugees and asylum seekers face various fundamental problems, such as having enough to eat and somewhere safe to live. Little attention may be given to the adolescent's social life, especially in a family where there are younger children to be cared for or where the English-speaking adolescent has to be the family spokesperson. However the adolescent's own social and psychological development is important. If they cannot join a peer group with positive and responsible attitudes and aspirations, then they may drift towards those with anti-social attitudes. Feeling lonely, insulted by the local population and persecuted by officialdom, the adolescent may find companionship with young people who break the laws of a community whom they believe have already rejected them.

Support for adolescent immigrants

Adolescent refugees may need help and support from youth workers so that they can meet peers and integrate. Norton (2001) suggests that the local youth service should:

- Consult with refugees and local agencies about providing support.
- Provide facilities for young refugees to include:
  - somewhere to meet
  - light refreshments
  - basic equipment for activities (sport, arts, drama, music)
- Find a source of funding.
- Provide ongoing support and access to other agencies and services.

- Encourage the adolescents to take responsibility for their group.
- Encourage adult refugees to become youth workers and undertake training.

Foster care moves

Adolescents in foster care may face frequent moves. Whether it is a response to behavioural problems or due to external circumstances beyond their control a move away from an established peer group can be a great loss. In his autobiography Dave Pelzer (1997) movingly recounts his early adolescent experiences of losing friends each time he moved foster-home and of not being accepted into established school peer groups. He teamed up for company with another outsider who turned out to be a budding delinquent. Despite his terrible experiences Pelzer had a resilient personality and just enough support to develop into a well-functioning adult, but many cope less well psychologically.

A quote from a girl in foster care shows the pain of having no friends and some of the reasons why she has given up making them:

> I've got a big space around me which is mine and nobody enters, and why...I don't know whether it comes from care having been let down so many times, or living with people for so many years and then going, and you never see them again, you build up a barrier to protect yourself...People try to break it to get in and you don't let them because you are so frightened it is going to happen again...I don't talk to many people...I never get to know people. I think sometimes the reason you never get anybody is because you want somebody so much that you never get them in that sense...when you get to somebody you cling to them so much you lose them, because they can't cope with the pressure you are applying on them. That comes from having nobody...once you've got somebody you think that it's mine now and nobody is going near him or her...and it's putting pressure on other people that they can't cope with.
>
> Stein and Carey, 1986: p137.

This speaks for itself. Such young people need long-term professional help and a stable environment.

Crises within peer groups

Just belonging to a crowd is not always problem free. Difficulties can arise within a group, leading to a social crisis for the individual. Muisener (1994) describes different sorts of crises which can cause a youngster to leave a group and trigger shock. These are:

- **The shock of exclusion**: the group demonstrates cliquish behaviour, ostracises and often scapegoats the member.
- **The shock of betrayal**: one crowd member is exploited by one or more of the others.
- **The shock of disillusionment**: often when a romantic relationship breaks up.

Any of these crises will cause shock and loss of self-esteem and an individual may go to great lengths to avoid the pain of peer rejection, shame or humiliation.

Some will turn to alcohol or drugs to numb the pain (see Chapter 10), others will hide themselves away from peers and others will find new companions, some with deviant behaviour patterns (see below).

Bad behaviour and deviant peer groups

Although the majority of adolescent crowds are not regularly involved in bad behaviour the crowd may overstep acceptable boundaries from time to time and a youth worker may need to intervene. Bad behaviour by an adolescent crowd attracts attention because antisocial 'gang' behaviour has detrimental effects for the local community. Most concerning are those crowds who regularly behave irresponsibly and break the law: the *deviant peer group*. Activities of such groups may focus around taking drugs, or daring one another to perform dangerous feats, or stealing for gain or fighting turf wars against other gangs. There are frequently serious consequences for the individual members and their psychological and social development may be adversely affected. Adolescents who belong to deviant peer groups need adult help although they may well be resistant to accepting it (see Chapters 10 and 11).

The troublesome adolescent and the deviant peer group

The individual who is troublesome and exhibits antisocial behaviour causes distress to those around them. Whether they are devoid of social skills or are hyperactive or aggressive towards others, they will soon be rejected by a 'normal' peer group. Research has shown that these rejected individuals nominate other rejected youngsters as their friends and are more likely to spend time with them as the only people available to them (Dishion, 1990). If, in addition, they receive little parental or adult attention or supervision they may well join a group of troubled and troubling peers.

The influence of the deviant peer groups also reinforces any maladjusted behaviour. Studies show that the main focus of such groups is their deviant behaviour: they discuss what they are going to do, they talk about how to do it and then act in a delinquent manner together (Dishion, 1990). It is the shared interest that keeps the group together. Their poor social skills may also be reinforced. Since none of them can model good skills for the others, the individual is unlikely to develop the necessary skills for acceptance by other groups. Such youngsters may benefit from intensive programmes as run by some Youth Offending Teams. Ideally some programmes should be aimed at 11 and 12 year olds before they begin offending and they should involve parents so that they can play an active role in monitoring behaviour too.

Sometimes the deviant group channels its aggression towards peers outside the group. As individuals the group members have low self-esteem but group-esteem rises if it perceives itself as stronger, more powerful or in anyway superior to an outsider. The victim is chosen carefully to ensure success and bullying results. Since this is a serious but common problem it merits a chapter of its own.

SECTION THREE: RECOGNISING AND RESPONDING TO CONCERNS

Chapter 9

Bullying

Bullying is a significant problem. This chapter defines bullying and explains how to recognise aggressive bullying, passive bullying and their effects on victims. A procedure for immediate intervention is suggested. Referral for entrenched bullying behaviour is advised.

Throughout children's literature from Flashman in Tom Brown's Schooldays to Malfoy and his sidekicks in the Harry Potter books, the bully and his entourage are familiar characters. Bullying behaviour is a worldwide problem among young people (Newman, Horne and Webster, 1999). Violent bullying tends to take place between boys and between girls. However name-calling, taunting, ostracising and isolating behaviour is also bullying and is just as damaging for the victims. It can lead to school phobia, depression, isolation and, in some tragic circumstances, suicide. Occasionally a young person will complain to an adult but mostly the victims suffer alone. The youth worker who can recognise the behaviour and begin some intervention can initiate a beneficial change for both victims and their bullies.

Recognising bullying behaviour

Bullying is persecuting, intimidating or hurting behaviour towards another person who is perceived as being weaker or inferior. An individual or a group may act negatively, repeatedly and intentionally, towards another, inflicting either psychological or physical harm, injury or discomfort. Newman et al. (1999) identify both direct and indirect bullying. Direct bullying involves open attacks on a victim, including threats or violence to the person or to their property as well as name-calling, taunting and open humiliation. Indirect bullying includes wilful exclusion from social groups. Olweus (1994) suggests three criteria which define bullying:

- Aggressive behaviour or intentional 'harmdoing'.
- Carried out repeatedly over time.
- In a relationship characterised by an imbalance of power.

Newman et al. (1999) also distinguish between 'aggressive 'and 'passive' bullies:

- **Aggressive bullies** may see themselves as fearless and tough and they are inclined to use violence. They need to dominate and to exercise power. They do not have empathy for their victims and they may distort the meaning of their victim's behaviour. As an individual an aggressive bully is likely to be impulsive and poor at interpreting social cues. For example: an accidental push is likely to be taken as a deliberate manoeuvre.
- **Passive bullies** do not instigate violence but they willingly participate. They are frequently insecure and anxious individuals who want to gain the approval, protection and friendship of the initiating aggressive bully. Unfortunately they admire their aggressive leader's social status and they are the followers who perpetuate the victimisation. Their socially excluding behaviour towards another can be mislabelled as just 'mean' or 'cliquey.' However it is bullying and it may have devastating effects on the victim.
- **Victims** may be insecure, anxious or sensitive individuals, but not necessarily so. Whilst boys are more likely to be subject to threats and violence, girls are more likely to experience social and verbal bullying (Sharp and Smith, 1991). Feeling weak and possessing low self-esteem, most victims are unlikely to retaliate and some will break down in fear and frustration. If they believe that their teachers, parents or peers have witnessed snubs but not intervened, then their feelings of worthlessness increase. Feeling abandoned a victim may not have even one solid friend at school and will try to stay out of the way. Chosen isolation may result with long-term harmful consequences.

Adult acceptance of bullying behaviour

In our culture there are popular television 'soap' characters who exhibit bullying behaviour but who are admired for their winning ways, while the harm that they do to their incidental victims is ignored. Similarly the young bully can also be a likeable and popular figure, admired by followers...and perhaps also valued by the youth leader because they ensure good attendance with the posse of groupies. There is also a social perception shared with the bullies that the victim is the cause of their own situation. 'It's the victims fault for not standing up for themselves, for being overweight, for being poor at sport, for wearing out of date clothes...' Unfortunately adults often stand by, unwilling to get involved, ignoring the harm and tacitly condoning the behaviour.

Dealing with bullying behaviour

The harm of bullying has been recognised during the 1990s and schools in the UK are now required to have policies for dealing with bullying behaviour. Children are being taught that this behaviour will not be tolerated in school and that the informer is not a 'tell-tale'. Older students with special training are often the workers who are able to confront the bully and help them to recognise the behaviour and its consequences, to consider the victim and to provide the impetus and the opportunity to change.

Appropriate intervention by the youth worker

Sometimes a youth worker has the opportunity to tackle bullying behaviour before it becomes established. When bullying comes to the adults' notice it has to be confronted.

Below is a suggested procedure for effective intervention; partly adapted from Newman et al. (1999):

Defusing the situation:
- Assume control.
- Demonstrate that you are taking the matter seriously by staying calm, moving deliberately and taking your time.
- In an assertive but not unfriendly manner ask the bully or bullies to wait at a convenient distance because it would be helpful to hear from them in a few minutes.
- Reassure the victim while helping them to retain dignity. Ask what happened and encourage some detail.
- Provide practical help and support and, if possible, find a mature peer with the social skills to respond appropriately to the victim whilst composure is regained.

Take time to prepare:
- Before addressing the bully or bullies, the worker must consider and control their own feelings of anger. If the intervention becomes a power struggle, the worker may win in the short run but this will only reinforce the experience that bullying 'works'. (The worker may use ultimate power to expel or exclude the bullies but then they will not learn and they are likely to find more victims. Do not threaten exclusion – but remember that it can be used if all else fails.)
- The worker must also deal with any feelings of fear based on their own past experiences of bullying. A bully will recognise the fear and use it to their own advantage.

Talking to the leader of the bullies:
- With a group of bullies, arrange to talk to the leader alone and in private but do this diplomatically, perhaps by asking for 'assistance.' They need to perceive the treatment as 'fair' from the beginning.
- Even though the feelings about the bullying behaviour are negative, the worker must feel positive about the bully as a person and their capacity to change.
- The long-term goal is to help the bully to learn self-control, some social skills in problem-solving and negotiation and to develop empathy for others.
- The short-term goal is to establish a relationship in which you can both talk and listen to each other's points of view about the behaviour, the feelings it generates in all concerned and a way to proceed in which no-one loses face.
- The youth worker needs to demonstrate firmness, a willingness to listen and a commitment to fairness for all, including the bully and the followers as well as the victim and all other group members.

- Talking with the bully requires:
  - a firm controlled voice
  - direct eye contact
  - open body language
  - time for listening
  - acknowledgement that they have valuable strengths but that they need to be used differently
  - discussion of the victim's perspective
  - a clear statement that the behaviour was actually bullying and that you disapprove
  - an openness about who needs to be informed
  - an offer of a dignified way forward – not backing them into a corner
  - an offer to continue the relationship (between youth worker and bully) – demonstrating ongoing commitment and your valuing of the bully

Talking individually to each bully:
- Talk to each of the followers in private, following the suggestions above. If appropriate acknowledge fears about losing friendships or becoming a victim.

All the above sounds a lengthy and difficult process but in practice it may take less than 10 minutes per person and the effort will certainly be worthwhile. Only the youth worker on the ground can tell whether an apology or reconciliation would be appropriate. If neither of these would be forthcoming a demonstration of a general change in attitude and behaviour would be the way forward.

The youth worker should alert colleagues to the situation and the way it is being handled. Ongoing support for the victim and the monitoring of the group behaviour must be considered. This may be an issue to take to consultant supervision.

Providing ongoing help

Group work with adolescents may reduce bullying and can be used by those experienced in working with groups. Gathering a small group of those who have been victims gives the participants the opportunity to find that they are not unique, to discuss the strategies for responding to bullying behaviour and to provide a source of mutual support. Newman et al. (1999) suggest that such groups should be same gender 'because boys may be embarrassed about describing their failure to cope with bullying episodes and their feelings of despair' (p333). Small groups consisting of both bullies and victims can also work therapeutically, by providing a safe environment where individuals get to know one another and talk about their experiences and feelings. However these sorts of groups should be organised by professionals with group counselling skills. A group for just bullies should be avoided as there is the danger that they might reinforce one another's aggressive behaviour.

Research has shown that bullying behaviour by an individual is a developing response both to biological and sociological factors, (Newman et al., 1999). Bullies frequently grow up in families where parenting is inconsistent and lacks warmth, where discipline is harsh and where aggression is tolerated. Unfortunately aggressively bullying schoolchildren do not grow out of their aggressive behaviour and the level of their aggression may increase unless there is some intervention. Where bullying behaviour is entrenched then *professional counselling, psychotherapy* or *family therapy* may be required for long-lasting effect. The youth worker should consult a supervisor, local agency or specialist organisation to work out the best approaches to the young person and their family, in relation to their particular circumstances. This is to increase the likelihood of co-operation and the young person's willingness to accept some help and to meet a counsellor or therapist.

Further information and contacts

Helpful organisations

Advisory Centre for Education (ACE)
1B Aberdeen Studios
22 Highbury Grove
London N5 2EA

Kidscape
2 Grosvenor Gardens
London
SW1 9TR
020 7730 3300
Website: www.kidscape.org.uk
Phone: 08451 205204

Website: Scottish Council for Research in Education: Bullying at School Information. http://www.scre.ac.uk

The 'No Blame Approach to Bullying':

Maines, B. and Robinson, G. (1992) *Stamp out the Bullying: Never Mind the Awareness, What Can We Do?* Portishead, Bristol: Lame Duck.

Chapter 10

Drugs and Alcohol: Users and Abusers

This chapter provides information about adolescent use and abuse of alcohol and drugs. It points out the acute and cumulative effects of drug-taking and factors which make some adolescents particularly vulnerable. It suggests how the youth worker may guide social users to change their behaviour and help abusers to seek professional treatment. Support for recovering abusers is also discussed.

Everyone working with young people today needs to understand adolescent alcohol and drug-taking behaviour because even if their own clients are not directly involved, they will certainly know young people who are. If a youth worker suspects that an individual or a group is experimenting with alcohol or cannabis, they should not ignore the situation. Without overreacting, which would be counterproductive, they should at the very least talk to them about the behaviour and aim to educate. However, suspicion that an individual or a group is 'abusing' substances or has any involvement at all with hard drugs requires the help of specialist workers. The youth worker may need to work initially with the young person to ensure that they will respond positively to a referral to an agency, health centre or specialist counsellor.

To act appropriately the youth worker must be able to recognise the vulnerable 'social user', the substance 'abuser' in need of professional treatment and the addict in recovery who needs support to reintegrate into a mainstream adolescent peer group.

Substances used and abused by adolescents

Adolescents use the same substances as adults. These include alcohol, amphetamines, cannabis, cocaine (crack), hallucinogens, solvents (including gases, glue and aerosols), nicotine, opiates (heroin), sedatives, hypnotic drugs and designer drugs.

(For a full list of substances and information about their effects, their legal status, chemical constituents and street-names see the NHS Health Promotion website: www.trashed.co.uk)

Defining 'use' and 'abuse'

For clarity in this chapter, **Use** means any involvement with substances, soft or hard drugs or alcohol, irrespective of the consequences. **Abuse** means involvement with substances which causes dysfunction or problems affecting an adolescent's physical well being, emotional well being, education, family life, social life or life in the wider community.

Muisener (1994) differentiates between adolescents with *substance use problems* and those with *substance abuse disorders*. While the former group may indeed face serious problems (expulsion from school, arrest by police, parental fury, incapacitating hangovers, fatal accident) they retain some control over their drug use. In contrast the individual with substance abuse disorder will continue to abuse despite the consequences. Even though the problems accumulate the adolescent will not be able to curb their behaviour because even 'these adverse consequences are more tolerable than discontinuing their chemical use' (Muisener, 1994: p12). This is the addict or alcoholic.

The four stages of teenage substance use

Macdonald (1984) describes the stages of teenage drug-using as a developmental continuum from experimentation to abuse as follows:

1. Learning the mood swing.
2. Seeking the mood swing.
3. Preoccupation with the mood swing.
4. Doing drugs to feel normal.

Muisener (1994) explains these more fully:

Stage 1: Experimental use. Learning the mood swing
The curious adolescent starts by experimenting to find out what others are finding enjoyable about a particular substance (and perhaps why parents and teachers are warning against it.) They find that ingesting the chemical substance creates a change of feeling, affecting mood or emotions.

The first effect may not always be pleasurable but, just as in other aspects of adolescence, they try to adapt to new feelings and gain mastery over them. Further experimental use leads to enjoyment of the mood swing effects.

Example: Whilst his parents are out 13 year old David and his friend drink a couple of cans of lager and half a bottle of cider left over from his parents' party. They are curious about its effects.

Acute problems: Even at this early stage accidents can happen. For the inebriated young person crossing the road and misjudging the speed of an approaching car, the consequence can be fatal.

Stage 2: Social use. Seeking the mood swing
The adolescent now finds like-minded peers who are also enjoying the substance-induced mood swings. The drug exploration and experimentation evolves into socially acceptable peer group behaviour. For some this is a normal and socially

adaptive stage of adolescence: undergraduate drinking is considered normal behaviour in the UK. Certainly not all adolescents using alcohol or drugs at the social level will progress to the next stage but there is a serious risk.

Example: Leo aged 15 has been regularly smoking cigarettes with his friends for the last twelve months. Three months ago they tried cannabis and now to stay in the crowd, Leo smokes cannabis each week-end. He once tried Ecstasy at a party and felt relaxed and happy.

For some, this is the beginning of moderate addiction. As they begin to develop tolerance so genetic propensity to addiction and neurological factors may combine.

Acute problems: Over-indulgence or a 'bad trip' can have some nasty effects, such as a chemically induced panic attack or a flashback. An accidental overdose can have fatal consequences. On the legal front, a young person may be arrested for possession of illegal substances or, with much more serious consequences, for supplying friends.

Stage 3: Operational use. Preoccupation with mood swings
This is the beginning of *abuse*, as the adolescent becomes an addict. Muisener describes two types of users:

- The pleasure-seeking 'hedonist' who seeks the chemical 'highs'.
- The compensatory user who is seeking temporary relief from painful feelings or from depression.

Both types may drink or take drugs a couple of times a week, but this is no longer a social experience. This adolescent abuser is now taking the substance for themselves and the company of others is less relevant.

Example: 17 year old Sharon's parents had separated two years previously and each had found a new partner. Sharon had started drinking when she felt depressed and then she started smoking cannabis too. She was then drinking each weekend, both with friends and alone, and smoking cannabis four or five days a week at home. She felt good when she was 'high' but for the rest of the time she remained depressed.

Acute problems: The likelihood of high risk behaviour increases whilst under the influence. The young person may react aggressively or violently to minor provocation, or risk unprotected sex or attempt suicide. Between episodes of using and intent on getting the next 'fix' they will break school rules or work rules.

Cumulative problems: Meanwhile the body is building up chemical tolerance. Brain functioning becomes impaired over more frequent episodes so that thinking and learning are affected. This impacts on performance at school, college or work and also on attendance and behaviour. Leisure activity begins to focus solely on chemical taking and non-drug-taking friends are neglected. Problems at home may become more frequent as families become aware and try to confront the drug-taking behaviour.

Stage 4: Dependent use. Using to feel normal
The addiction has a firm hold on the adolescent who now has compulsive urges to experience the chemical effects just to feel 'normal'. The ability to behave normally at school or work, to cope with the hiccups of everyday life and to maintain a sense of self are all drug dependent. At this stage the adolescent needs outside help and is very unlikely to be able to give up the drug-taking by themselves.

Case study: Aysha

Aysha aged 15 slept through many of her lessons. Her friends were concerned that they could smell alcohol on her breath each morning and she seemed to have lost her personality. They dragged her unwillingly to the school counsellor. After several sessions she admitted that she was drinking daily, taking hard spirits from her father's drinks cupboard. She was also spending all her substantial pocket money on alcohol, mainly vodka. She was an only child who was at home alone whilst her parents worked. They must have noticed that bottles of spirits were going down, for they replaced them, but they had never challenged her.

Acute problems: There is an increased risk of serious problems including medical complications and psychotic episodes, arrest for illegal activity to support drug habit, major conflict with family, peers or authority figures.
Cumulative problems: See below.

Signs and symptoms of substance abuse

Whilst most adolescents stay at stages 1 and 2, 6–10 per cent drift into stages 3 and 4. However even experienced therapists cannot differentiate between stages 3 and 4 for particular individuals.

From Muisener's (1994) detailed findings, the areas of life affected can be summarised as follows:

- **Physical health**: deteriorating physical appearance; sleep deprivation; weight change.
- **Psychological health**: poor coping resources; psychotic episodes; suicidal thoughts; impaired concentration, thinking and learning; antisocial behaviour becoming part of personality.
- **Behaviour**: increasing high risk behaviour including aggression and violence; promiscuity; accident proneness; suicidal behaviour; developing antisocial and/or illegal lifestyle.
- **Education or work**: increasing failure to attend; deteriorating performance; possible exclusion or dismissal.
- **Family life**: increasing conflict with parents and siblings; running away or being thrown out.

- **Social life**: rejection by non-substance abusing friends; seeking peers who will help with chemical abusing lifestyle; lack of interest in other activities.

Adolescents in stages 3 and 4 need professional help and the non-specialist youth worker or mentor can help most by getting the individual to seek that help (see Interventions below).

However recognising those individuals likely to become substance abusers and making timely interventions is a particularly valuable role that can be fulfilled by the alert youth worker.

Specific vulnerability factors

Young people who already have difficulties with their psychological development, family life or peer relationships are most likely to move from stage 2 to stage 3, (Allison, Leone and Spero, 1990; Muisener, 1994; Jaffe, 1998.) As these have been discussed in earlier chapters, just a few examples of particular difficulties that may trigger substance abusing will be given.

Impaired psychological development:
- Trauma caused by physical or sexual abuse in childhood or adolescence.
- Feeling different from peers due to faster or slower physical or sexual development leading to lowered self-esteem.
- Undetected learning disabilities (e.g. dyslexia) making adolescent feel stupid and so opt out or act out to disguise their difficulties.

Family life:
- Substance abusing parents.
- Family crisis: e.g. divorcing parents have to stay 'connected' to deal with adolescent son with drug problem.
- Long-term family dysfunction: history of neglect or parent with poor coping strategies.

Peer relationships:
- Peer crisis: rejection, bullying, exclusion from group, scapegoating experience or betrayal.
- Peer group involved with drugs: conforms to maintain group membership.
- Loner/outsider with no friends – joins group of other misfits all trying drugs and becoming a companion group.

Of the above Muisener (1994) suggests that the most vulnerable adolescents in need of specialist help are:

- Those with a current psychological disorder.
- Victims of physical or sexual abuse.
- Those growing up with substance abusing parents.

The youth worker with suspicions should not wait for more evidence before acting. Prevention is more effective than cure.

How to help

Before intervening the youth worker should be sure of their own position on drugs and that of their employer or organisation. Are they to follow a policy of harm reduction or complete abstinence? Is there anyone whom they are contractually obliged to inform?

Where they suspect that adolescents are exploring or experimenting with alcohol or drugs they may be able to call on a local drug treatment agency to send personnel with expertise in providing good programmes to nip the behaviour in the bud. Where there are no established links with local agencies the following drugs helpline website will provide contact information: www.lifeline.org.uk

A good programme may:

- Help the teenagers to learn about the effects of substance abuse.
- Help them to recognise their own problems.
- Help them to recognise their friends' problems.
- Give them access to resources and professional help.

Although this is specialist work the regular youth worker should get involved and work together with the experts. The young people already have a relationship with them and the programme will have more impact if they wholeheartedly endorse it and continue the work after the specialist team have 'flown out'.

Where an individual is regularly using in social groups and certainly where they have reached the stages of abusing, professional treatment by trained workers should be sought. Page (1999) lists the following options:

- specialist individual counselling
- family counselling
- group counselling or group programme
- full residential treatment

However, for a successful first-stage referral to an agency, GP or medical centre, the youth worker may well need to prepare the adolescent.

Preparation for referral

As in all other sorts of helping relationships, a trusting relationship has to be established.

In addition **some knowledge of drugs is essential**. An attitude of 'drugs are bad for you' is not enough. The youth worker has to establish credibility. The adolescent is likely to deny that there is any problem at all or that the substance abuse is having any effect on their well being or different areas of their life. The adolescent's family may be colluding in the myth that there is no real problem. The drug user may also try to debate the issues of drug legalisation and the evidence of harmfulness.

Choose a time and place where you will not be interrupted and when the user is not under the influence of drugs or drink.

1. Start by drawing attention to the behaviour that you have witnessed or the information that has been given.
2. Listen carefully to what they have to say.
3. Express your concern that drinking or drug using may be involved.
4. Again allow time for response but do not allow yourself to be fobbed off.
5. Explain your concern that substance abuse can get out of control and that you are concerned about their well being.
6. Listen.
7 Don't be surprised if all is denied. Remain attentive and respectful of their point of view. (Resist confrontation – see pitfalls below.)
8. Suggest that they might like to meet a particular worker who will provide information. How do they feel about that?
9. If negative (very likely on first approach), suggest that you might discuss this again.
10. Remind them that they are responsible for their actions and for the consequences.
11. Don't threaten. Just repeat that you will be willing to talk and listen again.

Your responsibility is not over. Discuss with your supervisor or a colleague when and how you should bring up the topic again.

Pitfalls

Progress towards referral may be slow but Page (1999) suggests ways of avoiding some of the pitfalls:

- Do not get into a debate about drugs. Listen but don't comment if they glamorise drug culture, or dismiss drugs as harmless. When they run out of steam, draw the focus back towards their behaviour or their feelings.
- Avoid answering whether you have ever tried illicit drugs. You will lose either way. If you haven't 'you don't know anything'; if you have, then 'you are no person to be lecturing them!' Explain that **they** are the focus of concern.
- If they get angry, do not respond with confrontation. This may be progress towards their accepting that they have problem (but don't tell them that!).
- Don't back away from any racial or gender differences between you. Talk about the difference. ('You don't understand that in my culture drug use is part of everyday life'. 'You're right! I don't know that much about your culture – but if you go to the agency, they are much more knowledgeable than me and could be more on your wavelength.') Do not suggest that you can refer to someone of the same race or gender unless you are absolutely certain of availability.
- Do not take any responsibility for helping the abuser to stop using. They can only stop if they are committed to doing so. You can offer no more than help with referral.
- Allow them to talk about their attitudes to their family, to authority figures and to their peers. Listen but do not encourage them to 'unpack' by asking leading questions or making interpretations. If vital information is disclosed

(e.g. history of abuse or bullying) contain the anxiety but do not explore. Get permission to pass it on at referral.

Page (1999) also warns that it is difficult to get abusers to accept counselling help. The youth worker should not feel a failure if the referral does not work. As in other youth counselling if you can establish a trusting first relationship they may be able to use the experience to develop another relationship when they are ready. Meanwhile if the adolescent is willing to hear about the range of programmes available to them, including self-help programmes such as Alcoholics Anonymous or other youth group projects, they might get the courage or motivation to visit one.

If there is a waiting list for treatment, the youth worker may need to maintain support during the wait, keeping the adolescent motivated.

Recovery and reintegrating into the community

The youth worker or mentor may also play a valuable role in supporting the recovering substance abuser. The adolescent who is being treated within the community may need an adult who, understanding the process of recovery, can be an encouraging listener and who can encourage 'sober' peers to engage with them.

Muisener (1994) describes four stages of recovery and the way that new friends can be supportive.

First stage: the shifting stage
The adolescent begins to tackle substance abuse when realising the harmful effects on their life. They are taught about the process of addiction. However they will have crises when they slip back to the habit and they may deny or rationalise these. At this stage they may not want to give up their old 'supportive' substance abusing friends and they may deny their bad influence.

Second stage: the sampling stage
As they can no longer rely on the 'substance' to provide them with inner resources (to relieve painful feelings or lift self-esteem) they have to look to others such as the therapist or parents to provide resources. This is a stage of painful struggle. They need to be actively involved in their treatment and to be committed to plans for recovery.

They may still be resistant to giving up their old peer group and not see that they may sabotage their recovery. However, group therapy may help as other recovering peers can challenge this behaviour and can provide genuine support. They will not make new 'sober' friends yet, either because they lack the social skills or because they are ashamed or fear failure.

Third stage: the conversion stage
They dare to become aware of their own feelings and they develope strategies so that they can express these feelings safely. They grow increasingly committed to their therapy programme. They will have longer periods of stability and sobriety but can still fall back and have crises. There may be periods of shame for past behaviour.

At this stage they are ready to start integrating back into their community and to attend school or college, or to go home if they have been in residential treatment. However they may find that that they have been rejected by their old peer groups. An ongoing treatment group may be invaluable for peer support. They may feel lonely as they try to find a new accepting 'sober' peer group. With this a youth worker may provide support.

Fourth stage: the coalescing stage
They make a commitment to maintaining their drug or alcohol free state. They have now built up their own inner resources and can also use the resources of their family. Their peer relationships become more stable and they begin to participate in mainstream peer culture.

Nevertheless a relapse may occur. The astute youth worker will not ignore signs of stress and will refer back to the therapist or treatment programme as necessary. Ongoing family support may need encouragement too.

Ongoing work for the youth worker or mentor

The mentor can be both role model and supporter. In addition to giving access to other professionals their role is to give clear and consistent messages about their own view on alcohol and drugs. If they are open to what may be happening in the local drug scene, the vulnerable teenager may be able to talk to them about how to avoid social drug-taking situations. Likewise the recovering abuser may be able to talk about temptations they have avoided, so gaining immediate reinforcement from their encouragement. Knowing that they are watchful and concerned and that they will act if the line is crossed may be a deterrent too. For some a trusting relationship and genuine concern may provide a turning point in deciding to stop using drugs and keeping to it.

Being in contact with local agencies and having some basic training in recognising the drugs themselves, their street names and their effects will strengthen credibility and confidence to act.

For further information

Alcohol concern: 020 7928 7377 / 4644 or www.alcoholconcern.org.uk
Drinkline (a helpline) 0800 917 8282
Website dealing with alcohol issues, info & advice www.wrecked.co.uk
National drugs helpline: 0800 77 66 00 or www.nationaldrugshelpline.co.uk
Drugs in schools helpline: 0808 800 0800
NHS Health Promotion website on drugs: www.trashed.co.uk

Further reading

Muisener, P. P. (1994) *Understanding and Treating Adolescent Substance Abuse.* Thousand Oaks, Ca: Sage.

Chapter 11

In Trouble: Criminal Offending

This chapter begins by describing the onset and nature of youth offending, the factors which combine to increase the risk of an adolescent offending and how the youth justice system deals with young offenders. The second part of the chapter looks at how youth workers and youth projects can help young people at risk of offending by maintaining trusting relationships. The third part stresses the importance of working with other services or agencies that help adolescents to change their behaviour.

By being alert to the factors leading to offending behaviour and being aware of the crimes adolescents are most likely to commit, the youth worker may be able to engage with the young person who is at risk of offending and deflect them towards more positive behaviour. A mentor may provide support for the persistent young offender who needs to change their behaviour and sustain new patterns of behaviour. By understanding the youth justice system and, in particular, the work of the local Youth Offending Team, the youth worker or mentor may be able to work alongside or co-operate with the other agencies that are involved in the young person's life.

Youth crime in England and Wales

Research using self-report and funded by the Home Office (Graham and Bowling, 1995) found that nearly 50 per cent of 14 to 25 year olds admitted to having committed at least one criminal offence. However, the majority of these individuals only committed one or two minor offences. Three per cent of young offenders accounted for 25 per cent of all the crime. Once an individual started to offend any positive influences of school or family began to decrease and the negative influences of deviant peers started to prevail. Although some young-sters started offending at the ages of 10 or 11, the most common age for adolescents to start offending was 15 years old.

Detailed information about offending by 11–16 year olds has been provided by MORI who conduct youth surveys annually on behalf of the Youth Justice Board for England and Wales. The survey undertaken from January to March 2002 (Youth Justice Board, 2002) analysed responses to questionnaires from 5,167 mainstream secondary school children and 577 pupils who had been excluded from school but were attending special projects. Of the mainstream pupils, 26 per cent responded that they had committed a criminal offence in the previous 12 months, while 64 per cent of the excluded pupils indicated that they had offended.

Gender differences

This survey showed that males were more likely to offend than females with 31 per cent of all male mainstream pupils and 22 per cent of all female mainstream pupils admitting offending. Of the excluded pupils, 69 per cent of the males and 49 per cent of the females had offended. The most common profile of a school age offender was a 14–16 year old white male who had been excluded from school.

Offending behaviour declines earlier in females as they become increasingly independent and acquire responsibilities (Graham and Bowling, 1995). Leaving school, getting jobs, leaving home to live independently, forming stable relationships and having babies all promote life changes which help females to desist from offending. For young men such social changes do not have a marked effect on their offending behaviour. For males, age tends to be the more significant factor; most of the men stop offending in their mid-twenties.

Types of offences

The Youth Justice Board (2002) reported that the most common types of offences committed by youths were stealing/theft (54 per cent) and threatening or assaulting someone (41 per cent). The most prevalent offences for mainstream pupils were fare dodging (46 per cent) followed by writing graffiti (34 per cent) and hurting someone who did not need medical treatment (33 per cent). Others committed criminal damage, dealt in stolen goods or stole things at school. One in five of them had taken drugs. Five per cent had stolen a mobile phone.

Individuals excluded from school were more likely to have committed a wider range of offences. The most prevalent were buying, selling or keeping stolen goods (60 per cent), hurting someone who did not need medical treatment (57 per cent), carrying a weapon (55 per cent), stealing (49 per cent), buying drugs for own use (48 per cent) and taking a motor vehicle without the owner's consent (40 per cent). Twenty five per cent reported that they had stolen mobile phones and 19 per cent had carried a gun. Those offenders who had been excluded from school were more likely to commit multiple offences, with an average of ten offences in a twelve month period, than those offenders in mainstream school, who committed an average of two offences within the same period.

Two thirds of all offenders (65 per cent) said that they usually offended with friends.

Drinking and drug-taking is involved in much offending (see Chapter 10).

Factors increasing the likelihood of offending behaviour

Some young people are considerably more likely than others to get involved in antisocial behaviour and then start offending. Several research studies (Graham and Bowling, 1995; Rutter, Giller and Hagell, 1998; Holman, 2000) suggest that the key 'risk' factors are as follows:

- Unsatisfactory parenting: parental neglect, erratic disciplining or poor supervision, lack of parental control.
- Parents who offend.
- Problems at school: disruptive behaviour at school, learning difficulties, underachievement and particularly truancy.
- Siblings who offend.
- Large family size: families with four or more children.
- Disrupted families and single-parent families: where parents have separated or divorced, where a single parent has poor coping skills (see Chapter 6).
- Low income/social deprivation: young people from low-income families, families relying on benefits and living in poor or socially deprived areas.
- Drug and alcohol misuse.
- Having been the victim of a crime.

While exposure to these risk factors does not inevitably mean that a young person will become delinquent, a combination of these factors working together will make a young person more vulnerable. An adolescent may be coping with a range of difficulties and remaining within the law until a particular temptation or a crisis occurs. On the other hand some adolescents offend when none of the predisposing factors appear to apply.

The youth justice system

The youth justice system deals with individuals aged 10–17 years, whilst those of 18 years plus are addressed by the adult system.

Responding to concern about youth crime, the government introduced the Crime and Disorder Act (1998) which stated that the youth justice system should prevent offending by children and young persons. To do this local authorities were given the responsibility for establishing Youth Offending Teams (YOTs) to co-ordinate the provision of youth justice services for all young people in their areas. Each YOT has to include social workers, probation officers, police officers and representatives from the education and health services.

The Youth Justice Board for England and Wales co-ordinates the system and its Chair, Lord Warner of Brockley, has stated that the mission of the youth justice system is to prevent offending. In order to do so the following principles must be implemented effectively:

- Early intervention in the lives of young people.
- Effective local systems requiring new ways of working together.
- Strong intervention by the Board where local agencies are failing.
- A co-ordinated approach across government to tackle youth offending.

Youth Justice Board, June 2002.

(For more information: http://www.youth-justice-board.gov.uk)

New forms of early intervention have been introduced. The old system of cautioning has been replaced. When a young person aged 10–17 years admits to committing a first offence, the police can deliver a 'reprimand'. For a second or more serious first offence the police give a 'final warning'. This warning triggers involvement by the local YOT who assess the youth and their risk of further offending and may institute a rehabilitation programme. If a third offence is committed the youth has to appear before a youth court.

In the youth court all sentences aim to prevent re-offending. Some directly address the causes of offending by, for example, monitoring regular school attendance to reduce truancy. Some orders provide parents with direction and support. Other orders require the young person to confront their behaviour, accept responsibility for offending, consider the consequences of their behaviour including the effects on their victims and make reparation. Following a change of practice in the youth courts from 2002 the youth magistrates ensure that each young person is fully involved in their court appearance and understands what will be required of them.

How youth workers can help

When working with an individual or group of young people at risk but not yet involved in offending, the youth worker may find it helpful to talk individually about:

- Behaviour that is actually breaking the law or approaching that level.
- Acknowledging responsibility for own behaviour.
- Understanding the implications and responsibilities of being a 'bystander' or accomplice.
- Consequences of the behaviour for:
  - the victims
  - the public
  - themselves
  - their own family
  - neighbours
- Friends who are involved in such behaviour and those who are not.
- Attending school regularly.
- Preparing for a job.

Avoiding pitfalls when working with vulnerable adolescents

Before starting to work with vulnerable young people at risk of offending read Chapter 2 if you have not already done so. It is essential that you work in a professional manner for the protection of both the young people and yourself. Consult your agency's policy and practice guidelines so that you are primed as to how to respond to ethical dilemmas, for example, admitting to offending behaviour or a situation involving abuse. Talk through possible issues of confidentiality with your supervisor or colleagues.

Maintaining relationships with an adolescent 'at risk'

Once a mentor has established a good relationship with a young person 'at risk', keeping in touch and maintaining that relationship increases the likelihood of positive influence. While each mentor has to develop their own way of keeping in contact, the following may be helpful:

- Remain consistent.
- Ensure that the young person knows how to make contact.
- Be willing to listen and respond with respect.
- Maintain positive belief in the youngster – that they have the capacity to change or to resist negative influences and so succeed in living a more positive life.
- Do not give up after failures – see it as another challenge and keep positive.
- Be resilient to negative behaviour and rejection.
- Where boundaries regarding behaviour are necessary, state them clearly and enforce them fairly.
- Before explaining a sanction, ask yourself whether you will be able to enforce it. Do not use empty threats. If you say that something will happen and you do not carry it out you will lose your credibility.
- Recognise and praise good behaviour, explaining what you see as the positive aspects to reinforce them.
- Co-operate with others working on behalf of the young person.
- Be visible – your presence may serve as passive protection against peer pressure.
- Encourage participation in community programmes or projects.
- Where relevant discuss small attainable goals. Together talk about how they could work towards the goal and achieve it. Follow it up: give praise when the goal is achieved but otherwise avoid negativity.
- When a pattern of good behaviour has developed, talk about your growing trust and allow sufficient space for the young person to feel empowered to take increasing responsibility for their own decisions and resulting actions.
- Maintain motivation in education – praise regular attendance and even minimal progress.
- Encourage keeping busy and making constructive use of leisure time – less time to get bored and find trouble. Give structured help with time management, such as writing out a weekly timetable for after-school and weekend activities.
- Maintain your own professional boundaries.

When confronting unacceptable behaviour:

- Before intervening double-check that the behaviour is really unacceptable. There can be just a fine line between offending and harmless mischief. (Challenge any prejudices of your own with your supervisor.)
- Change the emotional tone of the situation by lowering your voice, sitting down or moving away.

- If you are in full view or earshot of others, move yourselves to a more private place (but consider whether it is advisable to be alone with the adolescent – see Chapter 2).
- Ask what happened immediately before the behaviour or why it occurred and listen respectfully (however ridiculous or negative the explanation).
- Try to understand the behaviour:
  - Is the young person trying to say that the task or situation is too hard and is something they cannot handle?
  - Have they been embarrassed or made to look stupid?
  - Are they trying to test you?
  - Are they reacting to your gender, race or position – because past experiences with others have been disappointing, painful or confrontational?
  - Are they attacking because it is their best strategy of defence?
  - Are they trying to attract attention?
- Demonstrate that you still value them as a person but that it is the behaviour that is the problem.
- Explain why that behaviour was unacceptable and the possible consequences – to them and to others.
- Suggest another way of acting in a similar situation and ask for their suggestions and options.
- Use humour – but never sarcasm.
- Suggest that you meet again soon – so that you can both review what has happened today.

For other strategies and different approaches to managing difficult behaviour and encouraging positive behaviour see Ann Wheal's *Adolescence: Positive Approaches for Working with Young People* (1998).

Jason's case study illustrates how an astute mentor can see the danger signals early and take action. The young person can be helped to recognise that they may have to make difficult choices, particularly when under pressure from peers, but that they can learn to make safer decisions. They will also need continuing support so that they can sustain the new behaviour and then occasional support once the behaviour is established. The example also shows that this is unlikely to be successfully done by just one supportive youth worker. Often a whole team working within the community is needed to keep a young person occupied, motivated and monitored.

Making use of relevant agencies

If a young person 'at risk' is already involved with the local YOT then it should be helpful to liaise with them. They should know about the relevant family, educational and health issues and may be able to suggest ways of working or activities to complement the work they are doing. It is of no help to the young person to be pulled in opposite directions by those trying to help. A devious

Case study: Jason's big move

14 year old Jason was grumpier than usual when he sat down with George, his mentor, for their fortnightly meeting at school. However George soon managed to raise a smile at his own expense and Jason relaxed sufficiently to explain that he had been 'sent' to the Head of Year again. He had been provoked into a fight but as he had accidentally punched through a thin partition wall, he was the one who got all the blame. His punishment was a series of detentions, which he considered to be unfair and a waste of time. He finished his fighting speech '…but that Gavin had better watch out when I join the Stud's lot!'

George was alert. Before proceeding with the activity he had prepared he felt he should check out that final line.

G: What's that about the Stud's lot?

J: Oh, the Stud – he's a guy who lives down my way – knows what's going on – good to be on his side.

G: How's that?

J: He runs things – gets things organised and that.

From disjointed bits of information George managed to work out that the Stud was a 17 year old living a few houses away from Jason, who was head of a small local gang responsible for antisocial behaviour and probably into drugs. Jason wanted to join the gang – partly because he would then be 'respected' and also because he felt that he would be safer with them than on the outside. Mostly the Stud ignored him, but Jason was planning a 'big move' that would make the Stud notice and want him 'in'.

George was very concerned. Jason was a vulnerable lad with low self-esteem. Once involved with a gang he would have great difficulty extricating himself. He talked to Jason about the consequences of his actions and possible outcomes. While Jason could see a slight risk of getting caught by the police, he really could not grasp the other perspectives. The Stud was doing okay and he would too. However Jason also liked George and really looked forward to his one-to-one visits. George bought some time. He asked Jason to reconsider the 'big move' and said that he trusted him not to do anything until they met the following week. Jason agreed to keep out of the Stud's way until then.

George consulted his mentoring scheme supervisor. Jason's bad behaviour at school had been escalating, his single mother was unable to cope with him and his educational prospects were poor. He was already at risk of offending and joining a deviant peer group would be disastrous. The relationship with George seemed to be the only positive factor in his life. The supervisor suggested ways in which George could talk to Jason about keeping out of trouble and some examples, using TV characters, for putting gang behaviour into perspective so that Jason could understand more of the consequences and see fewer of the attractions. Meanwhile the school was encouraged to find work experience places for Jason.

With increased attention from George and the promise of a Saturday job, on the conditions that he kept some rules, Jason's self-esteem rose. For the time being he would keep away from the Stud and any possible trouble because he wanted that job…and George's approval…

young person may also pretend to different youth workers that they are working for the other one and so manage to duck out of co-operating at all.

'At risk' young people not covered by a YOT may be supported by other local schemes. A youth worker enjoying a successful one-to-one relationship with a young person may be reluctant to involve other agencies, in case they destroy their good work. However, a variety of support will usually be the most effective deterrent for that young person. Different agencies may focus on different aspects of the individual's life and also provide assorted time-filling activities. The bored young person is more likely to find trouble. Find out what youth projects are available in your area. There may be a youth project where youth leaders are available and with somewhere safe for young people to 'hang out' together in addition to organised activities. Also find out about the availability of 'ConneXions' which is a service set up by the government. This provides each individual with a personal adviser to liaise with different agencies offering personal development activities in areas such as sport, culture and job training. For more information see DfEE, *Connexions* (2000).

Providing projects that 'work': The Southdown Project

There have been some successful projects where youth workers have focused on particular groups of young people (Maychell, Pathak and Cato, 1996). Interviews of young people attending different projects indicated they most appreciated 'being listened to' and 'treated as adults'. The Southdown Project (Holman, 1981; 2000) is described here to illustrate different ways young people at risk can be given long-term support. This ongoing project, started by Bob Holman in 1976, was located on a council estate in Bath, where most families were poor and many had social problems. The youth leaders involved in the project actually lived in the community and the young people, originally 13–15 year olds, were regularly welcomed into their homes. Later the leaders gained premises where they could hold club activities but a greenhouse, attached to the Holman's family home, remained a place where young people could meet and could talk individually to the leaders if they so wished. Twenty or so years later Holman (2000) contacted 51 of the original young people, all then adults, to assess the long-term effects of the project on their lives.

These findings showed that the sustained support during early and mid-adolescence did have positive effects on later adolescence and young adulthood. Holman reported that, in a sample of 51 individuals, 36 had a combination of factors which indicated that they were at moderate or high risk of offending during their early teens. Between the ages of 16–19, of the 36 who had been vulnerable, 25 showed satisfactory behaviour, with low incidence of offending, lengthy unemployment, drug-taking or excessive drinking. This was better than would have been normally expected for such a group. Moreover, by 1999, 44 of the 51 were leading satisfactory adult lives, measured for the same factors, which was again statistically significant and better than would have been expected.

Holman described a variety of factors to account for the success of the project. In addition to providing standard club activities and an ever accessible meeting place, the same youth workers provided leadership for long periods and they won community and parental acceptance and support. Other helpful factors included co-operation with other agencies and the availability of jobs for the young people. However Holman suggested that it was probably the individual relationships between the young people and the youth workers which were central to its success.

Looking back at their involvement with the project, the interviewees reported that the most significant aspects of their relationships with the youth workers were that these leaders were:

- friendly
- approachable
- trusted
- living locally (therefore part of their community and not 'outsiders')
- good organisers (providing many activities which kept them occupied)

The relationships between the youth leaders and these young people developed when they were aged only 12–13. This set a solid foundation in preparation for the more challenging times:

> The most intensive contact happened at ages 14–15 when their personal and social diffi-
> culties loomed large at home, school and community. This was often the period when
> leaders were actively attempting to restrain the youngsters' behaviour, to control their
> tempers, to stop them fighting, to desist from truancy, to give up stealing. The result could
> often be tensions between leaders and individual youngsters with the latter perhaps
> storming out, verbally abusing the leaders and even physically threatening them. The
> relationships were at their most intense.
>
> Holman, 2000: p78.

The individual relationships he termed as 'resourceful friendship' (p78). Unlike relationships with social workers or teachers, these relationships were voluntary and the young people and the youth leaders did enjoy one another's company. However these youth workers also brought their skills and professionalism to the one-to-one relationships which were the 'core' of the project. Feedback from the participants twenty years later confirmed that they too believed that it had been the individual relationships with the youth leaders which had most positively influenced their lives.

Supporting non-offending siblings

Understandably, much effort is put into rehabilitating offenders and reforming the 'badly behaved' but often their siblings are given insufficient attention. They often require support to ensure that they do not follow a similar route into offending or because they are emotionally fragile.

Jane: the younger sister

16 year old Jane was regularly attending a course in hairdressing at her local further education college but she stopped going to her two-days-a-week work placement at a local hairdressing salon. The course co-ordinator, Ann, investigated. The owner of the salon had been pleased with Jane for the first month or so and, as far as he was concerned, nothing had happened to make her stay away.

Ann found Jane to be quiet and shy. Jane said that she was enjoying the course but that the salon 'wasn't right for her'. She asked about finding another salon in a neighbouring town. Ann was surprised as former students had always been happy at the present salon. She thought that Jane seemed depressed but could get little information from her.

Ann did not put Jane under pressure to attend the salon and she took different opportunities to chat to her. Trust grew. At one 'chance' meeting Ann asked if Jane's mother knew that she wasn't attending the salon. This time Jane was willing to talk about her mother and mentioned an older brother. It began to emerge that he was the reason for her reluctance to work at the salon. He could see Jane at work through the large front window. Although he did not live at home he would come to the flat to pester Jane for the money she earned in tips. He needed money and he was so intimidating that Jane handed it over. Anyway it wasn't the money so much as his behaviour. Her Mum always got so upset and so angry. Jane just couldn't face it, so it was easier not to go to work.

Jane needed ongoing support. Ann suggested that she consult her GP, since she was both unwell and depressed, and Ann also helped her to contact the local youth counselling service. This was a successful referral. As she gained in confidence, Ann helped her to transfer to another salon. Jane eventually gained her qualifications and left college but she dropped by to see Ann at college on odd occasions for a year or so just to let her know how she was doing (and to feel reassured that the support was still available.)

Hidden victims such as Jane do not know that they need support or that they are worthy of it. Many of them, whether members of families with troubles or living in areas prone to trouble, drop out of education or employment. The adults around them may attribute their non-attendance or poor work to 'bad attitude' or 'laziness' without recognising or bothering to find out the real causes of their difficulties. It is up to people working with adolescents to find out more and respond to their needs.

While intervention to assist youths in trouble used to be based on the assumption that problems came from within the adolescent, current understanding suggests that external circumstances play a role too (Leone, Walter and Wolford, 1990). Specialist help may be needed for addressing some of the following:

- family problems
- support for parents – so that they are able to manage an appropriate balance between maintaining control and encouraging independence
- educational needs
- health or sexual issues
- preparation for work experience or job-seeking

A twofold approach

To reiterate the main points of this chapter: firstly the youth worker needs to form and maintain a good relationship with a young person who offends or is at risk of offending before addressing issues of decision-making and changing behaviour. Secondly the youth worker should work with others to address those aspects of life which may continue to cause difficulty and may jeopardise all the progress made through the one-to-one relationship.

Adolescents need ongoing help if they are to gain control of their behaviour, make changes for the better, sustain those changes and become responsible citizens.

Useful contacts

To find your local Youth Offending Team: www.youth-justice-board.gov.uk/yot/index.cfm

Children's Legal Centre: 01206 873820

Chapter 12

Sexuality and Sexual Relationships

This chapter examines the issues relating to sexual development which concern young people. Puberty, forming pairs, decisions about embarking on sexual intercourse and safe sex are discussed. There is information about the transmission of sexually transmitted infections and HIV/AIDS with suggestions on providing support when a young person should seek testing. The final section discusses the development of gay identity and appropriate support.

Although concerns about sexuality and sexual relationships cause a great deal of anxiety, adolescents are frequently too embarrassed to discuss these worries with anyone. From childhood they have learned that some subjects are not openly discussed and so even finding the 'right words' may be a problem. Often parents are equally embarrassed and, once they feel that they have discharged their responsibilities by explaining the basic biological facts, they do not encourage ongoing dialogue. Meanwhile, when encountering puberty with its remarkable body changes and quite startling sexual feelings and mood swings, the confused young individual may wonder: 'Am I normal?' Shy comparisons with peers, or with what peers want to portray, may leave the individual lacking in confidence, but with nowhere to turn.

Conflicting messages abound. Educational programmes stress the risks and dangers associated with under-age sex; they also promote sex within secure, loving and monogamous relationships. However happily married couples who could act as positive role models keep their sexual relationships discreetly private. Teenage children may be embarrassed to witness any physical closeness between their parents. On the other hand the media provides lurid information about famous people having extra-marital sexual relationships. In television soaps teenagers having sexual relationships are commonplace, while teen magazines provide information about improving sexual relationships. Amid all this information, the sexually developing adolescent has to work out how to behave in relationships in their own socially changing world.

When a pairing forms between a girl and a boy, the early stages of getting to know one another by talking may soon be followed by a physical closeness which requires decisions regarding touching and kissing. While these decisions should be personal, there are often elements of peer pressure encouraging an individual to venture further than they really want to go. In addition internal physiological and emotional messages fight against all those messages of caution learned from parents and teachers. How far to go? And for the individual who begins to feel different but feels petrified because homosexuality appears to be shameful, what should they do?

Seeking support

Sometimes a crisis, such as discovering a pregnancy, prompts a direct approach for help but, more often, the approach is indirect. It is helpful to be able to recognise the variety of concerns about sexual orientation, sexual relationships, sexually transmitted infections (STIs), HIV and other sexually related problems which may appear in different guises. With some understanding of the different issues the support worker will have the confidence to respond to a hint or chance remark with both sensitivity and openness, sufficient to encourage the young person to talk just a little about the difficulties being experienced. Once the initial anxiety is contained, the adolescent may be able to acknowledge that there is a problem and to discuss ways of getting support.

The overall aim is to help the adolescent to develop healthy attitudes about sex so they can have fulfilling relationships, free of aggression and exploitation. In addition each individual should be able to take control within relationships, so that their life opportunities are not curtailed by unwanted pregnancies, HIV / AIDS or STIs leading to infertility.

Puberty

The physiological changes of puberty are the most visible signs of transformation from childhood to adulthood. The girl's body changes shape as she begins to develop breasts and pubic hair and she has her first menstrual period. The boy's genitals develop, he grows pubic and bodily hair and he experiences his first emission or wet dream. While most youngsters these days have been taught what to expect, whether from parents, friends or a sex education programme, the actual experience can still be a shock:

> *The onset of puberty perhaps takes boys less by surprise because male genital development is more visible. However, the recognition of sexual maturity may still be abrupt, as it was for Ted. He had been swimming with a group of boys during a holiday at the seaside. At the end of the day he was dragging his feet back to the shower, when suddenly he was aware that he **smelled** different: he smelled like a man. Horrified and confused, he dropped away from his friends and spent the rest of the holiday in a depressed and anxious state.*
>
> Noonan, 1983: p7.

The feelings, the smell and the mess are all unfamiliar and need to be dealt with by both boys and girls. The calm anticipation of a girl waiting for her first period, expecting to be in the bathroom at home within reach of her mother or older sister may be rudely shattered if she is camping in a field with a chemical latrine and primitive washing facilities.

Case study: My first period shouldn't have happened here!

The youth worker was alerted. 12 year old Helen was distressed and on the verge of tears. 'My first period shouldn't have happened in a field.' The youth worker checked that she had a supply of sanitary pads and that she knew what to do. However what she needed most was privacy from the others until she got over the shock.

The youth worker allowed her to express her disappointment. She had a stomach ache, it was messy and a nuisance. She had been looking forward to it because it was happening to her friends but she had really wanted to be near her mother. The youth worker suggested that she might want to phone her mother. The phone call was helpful to mark the rite of passage and, after more tears and some laughter, Helen felt confident to return to her friends. Nevertheless, after the rest of a happy camping week, the reunion with her mother was a tearful affair.

Giving an adolescent time and space may help with the adjustment. Some may need to mourn the end of childhood. They also need privacy. Brooks-Gunn et al. (1986) found that only about 25 per cent of girls tell anyone other than their mother about reaching their first period. Only later do they start sharing with friends and discussing the discomfort of periods.

Solitary sexual behaviour

Feelings of anxiety and guilt often arise with activities such as erotic fantasies and masturbation which may be the first forms of sexual behaviour that an individual experiences. Research suggests that while boys may talk with peers about masturbation, girls do not discuss it (Moore and Rosenthal, 1993). However both boys and girls are reluctant to admit that they masturbate because they perceive it as a shameful activity, particularly if they have been warned against it.

However self-stimulation does not cause harm and it may be enjoyable and reduce tension. Moore and Rosenthal (1993) suggest that expressed disapproval by parents can be more harmful to the teenager by affecting their psychosexual development. Masturbation may help the inexperienced young person to learn about sexual pleasure without entering a relationship until emotionally ready and accompanying fantasies may help to establish sexual preferences.

Masturbation only becomes a problem when it is performed to excess. If the young person avoids making relationships and is only interested in themselves, then this may suggest difficulties with sexual adjustment which may require professional help.

Sexual relationships

With the lengthening of adolescence, the time between first heterosexual relationships and the establishment of a long-lasting monogamous partnering leading to marriage and/or children is extending too. This period of time is much longer than it was a generation or so ago and this has increased the likelihood of premarital sexual intercourse. The age for teenagers to admit to having intercourse for the first time is decreasing. However there is still a sizeable minority who, for cultural or religious reasons, keep their virginity until marriage.

The range and variety of sexual behaviours is socially and culturally determined. Early adolescents tend to socialise in same sex groups (as described in Chapter 8) and meet members of the opposite sex in these groups at parties or informal meeting places. Older adolescents may socialise more in mixed sex groupings, but the pairing process is much the same. Kent and Davis (1993) asked 14–24 year olds to talk about one heterosexual encounter and most described a relationship which formed between the ages of 15 and 17 years. Being in a group of mutual friends helped a boy and girl to strike up conversation and have something to talk about. Sometimes they had seen one another previously and a friend had acted as a go-between to sound out how each felt before daring to make an approach. Friends could provide moral support or peer pressure. They stayed in a group at first, but eventually they separated themselves either by moving physically away as a pair to dance, to fetch a drink, to smoke or they were left alone by friends who drifted away as the couple tended to concentrate on one another. What happened next depended on what the authors termed as a 'social script'.

Kent and Davis suggest that a social script tells us what behaviour is expected in different social situations, for example when we visit a formal restaurant we expect to be shown to a table and given a menu. This social experience follows a preordained pattern. In contrast the social script of a heterosexual encounter has many variations – even if the end point is sexual intercourse:

> *Different paths lead to the same point, whether or not time is spent getting to know someone before having intercourse. Different tracks range from fast (one-night stand) to the slow (courtship rituals and marriage); from the unplanned (waiting until the time is right) to the planned (seduction) and there are many obstacles (lack of privacy, errors of interpretation) to interrupt the flow.*
>
> Kent and Davis, 1993: p5.

Although the script is far from clear, most young people are unlikely to talk about the possible relationship itself when they have just met. Neither knows what the other is expecting nor perhaps what they each want for themselves. They may rely on non-verbal behaviour but they might misinterpret one another's cues. Not surprisingly the whole situation may be fraught with anxiety for the inexperienced adolescent. Once within the encounter they may forget that each have responsibility for what happens next and can take control. The individual who has thought through possible situations or, better still, talked them through beforehand is more likely to have the skills to keep control.

Support from youth worker or mentor

The youth worker or mentor who already has a trusting relationship with a young person is sometimes given an indication about relationship worries.

Case study: Am I interfering?

Tanya arrived for her mentoring session with a big smile and an air of excitement. Her mentor, Cathy, felt pleased that the shy, naive 14 year old was at last gaining confidence. Cathy had been helping her with literacy skills and this had had a knock on effect. Now Tanya was making friends and going around with a posse of girls. In conversation Tanya divulged that the boy she really fancied was going to be at the club on Friday night and that she hoped he was getting interested in her.

Although this was all very innocent and normal, Cathy was aware of Tanya's naivety and felt some concern. However, this was none of her business.

For a few weeks Tanya was positively bouncy and learning well. Then, some six weeks on, she arrived looking dejected and was unable to concentrate. With tears trickling down her cheeks she confided to Cathy that Dave had 'gone too far' and she would never trust a boy again. She did not even feel she could face the other girls and that there was just no point in making friends after all. Cathy shared in the sadness and helped Tanya to make an appointment with a counsellor. However she had the nagging feeling that she might have been able to prevent something – if only she had 'interfered' earlier.

What could Cathy have done?

The mentor who really gets to know a young person builds up a trusting relationship. If the young person starts to talk about their life outside the focus of their work together then there is permission to enter into a dialogue. However the mentor must remember that this relationship is purely for the benefit of the young person and not to satisfy their own curiosity or any other of their own needs. This is not permission to be a 'voyeur'.

With this in mind the mentor can allow a dialogue to open. An open question can indicate willingness to listen:

Do you want to talk to me about your friendship (relationship) with…(person's name)?

Although the initial approach may be declined, a week or two later the adolescent may mention the relationship again and then accept the invitation to say just a little more. If the mentor remains non-intrusive the adolescent may be able to talk about feelings and about the sort of relationship that they want.

The overall aim of intervening is to support healthy sexual adjustment which will enhance life satisfaction. The following may be helpful:

- Each young person needs to find their own personal path in each intimate relationship. They should not be pressured by the other partner:
  - *If you really loved me, you'd want to do it.*
  - *It's a sign of your commitment.*
- There are points of choice when a person can agree or say no about going further (kissing, touching, fondling etc).
- There are ways of talking to a partner and negotiating. Issues may include: how far one is prepared to go, the nature of the relationship, the use of contraception.
- Cultural context and local youth culture will both influence a young person's value system regarding sexual behaviour. For some individuals premarital sexual intercourse will be strictly taboo while for many it will be permissible or even desirable at a particular stage in a relationship. However an individual may choose not to go along with the cultural norms for their group. They should not be pressured by friends:
  - *Everybody does it, so it must be right.*
  - *By my age no-one else is a virgin.*
  - *I won't be part of the crowd.*
- In many cultures double standards for boys and for girls persist: casual sexual activity for boys is acceptable (and may enhance a reputation) whereas casual sexual activity for girls is prohibited (and may damage a reputation).
- Sex can be exploitative and used to gain power.

Talking about the sort of problems that young people face in relationships, may help the individual to gain sufficient confidence to communicate how they feel to a partner and/or to make some decisions about how to proceed with a relationship.

In addition you may feel confident about giving advice on:

- all methods of contraception
- sexually transmitted infections (STIs), HIV / AIDS
- local sexual health clinics

For this you do need to be fully informed and up-to-date.

Caution

Before intervening you need to think about your own value system regarding adolescent sexual behaviour. Will your interventions be reflecting your own beliefs and will it be right to do so? Are these in line with the stated policies or known beliefs of the organisation to which you are affiliated (e.g. church, school, youth movement)? Ethical and moral dilemmas can be discussed with your supervisor. If you feel ambivalent about discussing sexual behaviour then the adolescent will sense this. Instead you can help to make an appointment at a sex counselling centre or youth counselling service.

Sexual intercourse: protection from sexually transmitted infections and HIV/AIDS and pregnancy

Despite good health education programmes which cover both the positive aspects of sex and the dangers of HIV/AIDS, sexually transmitted diseases and unwanted pregnancy, many adolescents still have unprotected sex. Young people may know all the risks in theory but studies regarding the sexual behaviour of young people (Cragg et al., 1993; Dockrell et al., 1993; Kent and Davis, 1993) show that this knowledge is not reflected in their sexual behaviour. Rosenthal et al. (1996) describe myths and stereotypes which affect young people's decisions whether or not to have safe sex. Below are some beliefs which encourage unsafe behaviour:

- Young people believe that if partners look healthy and have healthy lifestyles then they are likely to be clean and therefore risk-free.
- If couples meet through mutual friends, each feels that the new partner is actually 'known' and is therefore 'safe' i.e. free from infection.
- Because casual sex is frowned upon for young women (double standards – see above) a girl may only consent to sex when the relationship is one of 'love'. Love assumes trust in a meaningful relationship; using a condom is interpreted as denying trust.
- Men are expected to have sexual urges and to take the lead in encounters. The girl is expected to take some responsibility for her own protection. However if she states too early that she will only have sex with a condom she may be flaunting her availability.
- If a girl produces a condom such preparation may be interpreted as promiscuous because she is anticipating casual sex.
- Sex is more enjoyable if it is spontaneous and condoms can ruin the spontaneity and the romance.
- A condom spoils the enjoyment: 'like having a shower in a raincoat.'
- The rewards of condom-free sex are immediate enjoyment and gratification whereas the possible outcome of STIs or HIV seems distant and unlikely to happen 'to me!'
- Once a relationship has developed a girl may go on the pill and they will stop using a condom. She is protected from pregnancy and since they now are in a 'love' relationship, concerns about STIs etc. would be offensive.
- Since the vocabulary of sexual language is very close to colloquial vulgarity, couples may not find an appropriate set of words to discuss their sexual relationship and then never discuss it all.
- Some are completely misinformed and believe that HIV will only be caught via homosexual intercourse.
- For some, taking a risk enhances the enjoyment.

- Since condoms can split and are not 100 per cent effective, they may be discounted as generally useless.

Occasionally an anxious young person will confide that they are contemplating sex for the first time or that they are practising unsafe sex. They may feel unable to get out of a bind because of a mixture of the beliefs stated above. The youth worker may offer the opportunity to talk about what they are doing, to dispel some of the myths and to consider the risks and possible consequences if their practice continues (see below). This may be sufficient to provide the motivation to take control and change their behaviour.

Sexually active young people need to understand that sexual intercourse carries the risk of STIs (see below) as well as unwanted pregnancy. While pregnancy is regularly considered, STIs including HIV somehow seems irrelevant. Unprotected sex gives immediate pleasure while the infection (STI) that may follow is only obvious later and in the case of HIV will take months to develop. The youth worker can suggest ways of modifying lifestyle to reduce risk:

- Always using a condom or diaphragm (in addition to the pill).
- Practising non-penetrative sex.
- Reducing the number of sexual partners.

Being in possession of the facts can bolster the credibility and confidence of the adviser.

Sexually Transmitted Infections (STIs)

The incidence of STIs is rising dramatically among teenagers in the UK but many sexually active young people are unaware of the risks and the consequences. *Chlamydia* is one of the most common STIs in the UK. If it is left untreated in a young woman it can lead to pelvic inflammatory disease (PID), future fertility problems, ectopic pregnancy or chronic pelvic pain. STIs are usually passed from one infected partner to the other by sexual intercourse (vaginal, anal or oral) but different STIs can be passed in some other forms of intimate touching too. The other most common STIs in the UK are gonorrhoea, genital herpes, genital warts and HIV (see below).

STIs should be treated medically as soon as possible because their consequences, if left untreated, can be so serious. Young people should be helped to make an appointment at their local sexual health clinic (see next section).

HIV and AIDS

HIV (Human Immunodeficiency Virus) is an STI which can turn into AIDS (Acquired Immune Deficiency Syndrome) which may be fatal. Although the number of people dying of AIDS has been falling, the number of individuals in the UK being infected with HIV is increasing. Young people need to know this.

HIV is transmitted in the following ways:

- Heterosexual or homosexual intercourse – through infected semen, vaginal fluid, anal or oral intercourse.
- By sharing infected needles, syringes (as for drug-taking).
- By infected skin-piercing instruments (tattooing, ear-piercing).
- By transfusion of infected blood or blood products (in the UK there is donor screening and heat treatment, but those travelling abroad need to be aware).
- From mother to baby, during pregnancy, at delivery or after birth by breast-feeding.

Transmission of HIV infection can be prevented by:

- Avoiding unprotected vaginal, anal or oral intercourse.
- Using condoms, spermicide, diaphragm or cap with care.
- Using only clean needles, syringes and other equipment.
- Not donating blood if potential donor or donor's partner may have been at risk of HIV.

Adapted from Bor, Miller and Goldman, 1992.

If a young person believes that they have been at risk for HIV they should be very strongly encouraged to attend a clinic or sexual health centre for testing. The youth worker can ease the way by explaining the exact location of the clinic, clinic opening times and what to expect.

Talking about testing for HIV/AIDS

One way of beginning is to ask:

What do you know about HIV or STI clinics?

You can explain that confidentiality is a high priority. The staff working in such clinics will be specialists who will treat them with respect and be non-judgemental. Before any testing there will be pre-test counselling so that they understand the process and what everything means.

Do you know how they test for HIV?

It is a straightforward blood test. The results are not immediate. You will be told when you are to come back and receive the results. Normally these will only be given personally and not given by post or over the telephone.

The youth worker not qualified in sexual health counselling should not attempt to provide the information about HIV testing and results. However a very scared adolescent may need to know that HIV does not always develop into AIDS and that there are now anti-retroviral drugs which can delay the onset of AIDS. The youth worker's role is just to prepare the young person sufficiently so that they will get to the clinic with sufficient confidence to get through the door and see an adviser. The youth worker may want to check that the adolescent attended but not pry further.

I am not going to ask about what happened, but do you want to tell me whether you actually saw someone at the clinic?

Once the young person has attended, the role of information-giver is over although the supporting role may continue.

For helpful, clearly written information: www.lovelife.uk.com

Also see www.youthinformation.com

Click on: family and personal relationships

Developing gay or lesbian identity

While all young people have to face the varied physical, emotional and social challenges of sexual development, some have the additional challenge of determining their sexual orientation or identity. The first feelings may be of being 'different' from peers, without quite knowing why. Then in early adolescence they might gradually realise that whilst the majority of their peers are attracted by the opposite sex they are developing same-sex attractions. Owens (1998) describes 'becoming' gay as a four-step process: from feeling different, to becoming aware of same-sex attractions, through engaging in same-sex erotic behaviour and dating and finally to self-identifying as gay, lesbian or bisexual. Many young gay people and their families manage to adjust positively to their sexual identity without outside assistance although some do require professional intervention. However easy or difficult the process a young person may appreciate support from a sensitive, understanding and independent adult.

Being different

Adolescents generally like to conform with their peers, so discovering that one is different can be most uncomfortable. Gay young people often feel that they do not fit in with others in their age-group and so find it difficult to go to school or join in youth activities, such as team sports. Others such as high academic achievers may find solace in studying hard and find sanctuary in the classroom (Barber and Mobley, 1999). Many find themselves shying away from forced heterosexual socialisation such as the 'school disco' or even the canteen. They can become isolated.

Young people are also fully aware that there is a mainstream cultural assumption of heterosexuality (Barber and Mobley, 1999). From quite a young age they are conscious of anti-homosexual messages. The young person who begins to wonder about their own sexuality may be fearful of rejection or alienation. They might be particularly worried about disclosing personal feelings or of others noticing the difference. Some might have their fears confirmed by witnessing or by being the butt of homophobic reactions or by experiencing threats or harassment.

Confusion about sexual identity and homophobic pressures frequently engender feelings of shame and guilt and these can lead to depression or self-hatred. Barber and Mobley (1999) report that gay male youth are more than twice as likely to commit suicide than other male youths. Some escape their feelings by abusing drugs or alcohol. There are also dangers when young gay people feel inclined to experiment sexually. As there are few meeting places for young people they may visit adult venues, bars or clubs, where they are in danger of exploitation and of sexually transmitted infections including HIV. Some gay adolescents have 'anonymous sex with older men or trade sex for drugs or money' (Barber and Mobley, 1999: p165) because they do not know that there are other gay options. They may never realise that same-sex relationships can be positive and that they too are entitled to emotional intimacy within a positive, safe and secure relationship.

Supporting positive adjustment

Most gay young people do become well-adjusted adults, well-integrated within society. Those coming into everyday contact with these young people during their adolescence can help by providing a safe and supportive environment in this often unsafe world. Ideally they should have access to counselling or mentoring, places to meet other young gays and provisions, such as condoms, for safe sex. In the UK the legal age of consent for homosexual intercourse is 16, in line with heterosexual intercourse.

Sometimes a youth worker in conversation with a young person may sense that sexual identity is a concern and may really want to help. It is important that the youth worker is aware of their own feelings about homosexuality and that they can accept individuals with different sexual orientations. Owens suggests that even a mildly homophobic counsellor may try to 'change' a youth and that is likely to be counterproductive or even harmful. The adolescent may need to explore their sexual orientation, for it may not be settled, with someone who can be sensitive, caring and genuine but who also knows about:

> ...myths and realities surrounding homosexuality, causal theories of sexual orientation, legal implications, the coming-out process, attractions, disclosure to non-significant non-gays and the need to do so, positive identification as lesbian or gay, vulnerability of lesbian and adolescent gays at the point of disclosure and high risk sex and HIV transmission.
> Owens, 1998: p171.

The non-specialist youth worker cannot expect to have such detailed knowledge but they can be the first step for the youth in gaining the sort of support that is needed.

Homosexual identity formation

The stages of sexual identity formation are similar to those for other identity formations. (Compare with cultural identity formation in Chapter 7.)

Case study: Steven – a depressed student

17 year old Steven consulted a support tutor, Janet. Although he had been a good student, half way through his A level course he found himself demotivated and unable to concentrate. He was anxious not to lose his chance of getting to university. Janet helped him to organise his workload but also talked with him about his loss of motivation. He mentioned that group work projects were difficult as he felt a bit of an outsider and tended to take a marginal role, even though he was one of the more able group members. Janet learnt that Steven had only one friend, Tim, and, apart from a supermarket job, his pursuits were solitary.

Although Steven was making progress with his work, Janet was concerned about him. He seemed depressed but said that he did not want to visit his GP. At their fourth weekly meeting Janet was making general conversation. Steven talked a bit about Tim, explaining that they were both outsiders and that they had similar problems. Janet recognised an invitation to ask more and wondered whether Steven wanted to say more. However she felt somewhat unprepared for the remark that his relationship with Tim was 'not sexual or anything but we just talk.' Janet consciously controlled her body language as she absorbed the message that Steven's problems were around sexual matters. His demeanour of acute embarrassment mixed with a sort of defensiveness told her that she had stumbled upon a serious difficulty. She had sufficient experience with adolescents to know that her reaction now would have significance. She kept her tone light and wondered whether he might want to talk about this some more. He was silent. She allowed the silence for a few minutes and then nodded, broke the silence and returned to his academic work. She wondered whether he would return the following week.

He did return and over the next few weeks he talked about being fairly sure that he was gay. Some months ago he had told his mother, with whom he had a poor relationship. His mother had reacted angrily and with disbelief for she had been unable to accept his disclosure. Talking to Janet had freed Steven. He was suddenly able to socialise with others in his class, particularly a couple of girls. Over the next couple of months he even shared serious conversations with them. However Steven had never had a sexual relationship. He wanted a relationship but he did not know how to meet other young gays. He was also aware of the dangers of 'just getting picked up.' Janet was able to get advice from a youth counsellor whom she consulted and she gave Steven information about a local organisation and the Gay and Lesbian Switchboard.

Knowing how to get support and the possibility of meeting others was a great relief. In the end Steven decided to go no further until his exams were over but he continued to meet Janet every two or three weeks. He visited Janet once more after he had reached university to let her know that he had joined a Gay and Lesbian Group.

Within the trusting relationship Steven felt able to disclose his concerns over being gay and Janet was able to use her sound basic counselling skills to make it a good enough experience. She provided the time and place to explore thoughts and feelings which enabled him to start the process of adjustment both by integrating back into his age-group and finding out about meeting others. The process was unhurried. Janet had plenty of time to get the information that she needed for Steven and also to get support for herself, since this was a new area for her too.

Cass (1996) suggests the following six stages of development:

Stage 1: Identity confusion
Mismatch between present sexual feelings and an old view of self as a hetero-sexual, together with concerns about homophobia.

Stage 2: Identity comparison
Feeling different. Comparing self with others to work out own identity and reading gay material to find out about others sharing similar feelings.

Stage 3: Identity tolerance
Establishing contacts in the gay community – but still presenting self as hetero-sexual in non-gay environments.

Stage 4: Identity acceptance
Comfortable with being gay in some situations. May 'come out' to close family and close heterosexual friends.

Stage 5: Identity pride
Feel proud about being gay. Seeks activities and environments to nurture and support a gay orientation. May show anger towards those heterosexuals not accepting gayness.

Stage 6: Identity synthesis
Willing to disclose gay identity to anyone and able to deal with both positive and negative reactions. Gay orientation is now recognised as just one part of their personal and cultural identity. Homophobia can still cause anger but it is not as intense as in stage 5.

A young person will move back and forth between these stages and may be content not to move beyond stage 4. Often there are difficulties around stage 3–4 with 'coming out'. Outside support may be needed at this point.

Coming out

Coming out is a very important but slow process: it is not a one-off event (Owens, 1998). The adolescent needs to be fully prepared for all sorts of reactions, particularly when coming out to parents. They should talk through possible consequences both for themselves and for their parents:

- How might a parent react?
- If the reaction is bad / rejecting, is support available?
- Might you be thrown out of home? If so, where will you go?
- Is this the best time? (Not before exams, family wedding, parent going on holiday).
- Who could give support to your parents or to you and your parents together?

The youth worker may not have the time or experience to provide the necessary support. In most cases referral to an organisation with expertise in this field is the safest and most helpful option.

Referral for specialist counselling

In addition to getting support for coming out, some may also need specialist support. These include those who are experimenting or acting out with unsafe sexual behaviour, substance abusers and those who appear particularly unhappy or distressed. Experienced counsellors can help with the following:

- Exploring gay identity development.
- Helping a young person come to terms with their own homophobia.
- Restructuring a negative self-image.
- Learning assertiveness skills to combat homophobia.
- Social skills training for 'coming out'.
- Ways of using support networks to bolster coping skills.
- Integrating being gay into an individual's whole cultural and personal identity.

Adapted from Barber and Mobley, 1999.

Further information

Websites:
AVERT: www.avert.org/yngindx.htm

www.youthinformation.com
Click on 'family and relationships', then click on 'family and personal'

Helpful contacts

Lesbian and Gay Switchboard. Tel: 020 7837 7324

Out on Thursday: An online service for gay young people:
ralph@outonthursday.freeserve.co.uk

Chapter 13

Teenage Pregnancy, Teenage Mothers and Teenage Fathers

This chapter raises the issues surrounding teenage pregnancy and the ways to encourage young women to get specialist advice and support. With unwanted pregnancies, decisions have to be made. There are also short sections on giving occasional support to teenage mothers and to teenage fathers.

Pregnancy

When contraception fails or is not used for any of the reasons discussed in the previous chapter, pregnancy may result. Some girls do not realise that they are pregnant and some deny it, hoping that it will just go away. Others are able to tell their mothers, partners, other relatives or close friends and so get necessary support and care. However a sizeable proportion of newly pregnant young women feel unable to confide in family or friends and some seek out an outsider whom they can trust to keep their confidence and to whom they look for immediate advice. The youth worker or mentor receiving such a disclosure can be helpful both by providing immediate emotional support and by acting as a stepping-stone to appropriate professional support for decision making.

Emergency contraception

The young woman wishing to prevent pregnancy within 72 hours after intercourse can be advised to go immediately to a GP or family planning clinic and to ask for emergency contraception. The two types of contraception are hormone or 'morning after' pills (not to be used as a regular form of contraception) and the Intra-Uterine Device (IUD) or 'coil'. The IUD must be fitted within 5 days of intercourse taking place, to prevent the fertilised egg from attaching to the uterus. The Brook Advisory Centre (Donnellan, 1997) reports that emergency contraception fails to prevent pregnancy for 2 per cent of women who use it.

Planned pregnancies

Studies of teenage mothers have shown that some have planned their pregnancies. Figures vary but studies of young mothers in the UK in the 1990s suggest that between 18–25 per cent had planned to have a baby (Phoenix, 1991;

Hudson and Ineichen, 1991; Allen and Bourke Dowling, 1998). Of this group a few were married and many were in stable relationships with their boyfriends at the time of conception. However, in a study of teenage mothers, Allen and Bourke Dowling found that by the time the babies were a year old, half of the women were no longer in a relationship with their baby's father. They also found that even when pregnancies were pre-planned by the mother, over half of them had not discussed their plan to have a baby with their partner beforehand.

Some teenage women want a baby to fill the void in their own lives; some are repeating their family history of teenage motherhood. Beforehand they are unlikely to consider whether they have reached a stage of maturity in which they could provide all that a child requires and most do not look that far ahead. Nor do most think through the practicalities of where they will live or how they will support themselves. Contrary to widespread political opinion in the late 1990s, they do not choose to become pregnant in order to benefit from local authority housing (Allen and Bourke Dowling, 1998).

Young women content with their pregnancy should be encouraged to:

- Seek an early appointment with their GP or local clinic so that they receive all the care and essential information to promote a healthy pregnancy and birth.
- Discuss the practical issues of living accommodation, financial provision and available benefits so that they are as prepared as possible. Teenagers may be lacking in confidence themselves and may need help making initial approaches or working out appropriate questions.
- Be assertive but calm and polite when dealing with statutory agencies. Procedures can be slow and lengthy and frustration is a regular hazard. They should not assume that 'they' alone are being victimised. They should be organised with their own paperwork. (If all official letters and documents are put straight into a box-file when received, they will be safe and available.)

Unplanned pregnancies and decision-making

Most teenage pregnancies are unplanned and are initially unwanted events.

In the early weeks of pregnancy a teenage girl in the UK can decide to:

- Give birth to her baby and to bring it up, with or without support from her family and the father of the child.
- Give birth to the baby and agree to adoption.
- Have a termination of pregnancy as allowed by the Abortion Act (1967).

Keeping the baby

Many young pregnant women do not consider that they have a choice. Obviously, if they do not take action and make a decision, then their pregnancy will continue. Many believe that once a girl is 'caught' by a pregnancy she should give birth to the baby and bring it up. In some social groups, social pressure enforces that because terminating a pregnancy is regarded as 'selfish'. Interviews of teenage mothers by Hudson and Ineichen (1991) showed a very wide range of reasons for the girls deciding to keep their babies. These included ignorance or denial of the pregnancy, wanting an object of love, wanting something to do, hoping to keep the boyfriend as a partner, rebellion against parents, confirming a self-fulfilling prophecy that she is a 'bad lot', encouragement from her own family who are ready to welcome another baby, negative pressure about getting the baby adopted, getting bad advice about the availability of abortion and being afraid of medical intervention. Many teenage mothers do not disclose until they are late on in the pregnancy when termination is no longer an option.

Adoption

Adoption is the least favoured option and is now rare in the UK. Most young women see this too as 'selfish' or intolerable and feel that once they have had the baby they would be unable to give it up (Allen and Bourke Dowling, 1998). Hudson and Ineichen suggest that a girl has to be mature and confident in herself to be able to make such a decision and keep to it. They give some illustrative case studies where adoption was the route followed and some time afterwards the mother still felt that she had made the right decision. They suggest that adoption may be generous as well as selfish.

Abortion

Up to the 12th week of pregnancy, abortions can be performed by removing the contents of the uterus by suction. This can be done under local or general anaesthetic. After the 12th week and up until the 24th week abortion involves removing the contents of the uterus by instruments.

UK government public health statistics show that in 1999, of the 92,400 conceptions to young women under the age of 20 in England, 39 per cent were terminated by legal abortion. Of the 7,400 conceptions for girls under 16, 53 per cent were terminated by abortion. The percentage of abortions each year has been gradually increasing (Department of Health, 2002).

Some young women make the decision to have an abortion and do not suffer afterwards while others find that the consequences are unsettling and emotionally painful. Sometimes a second pregnancy follows an abortion 'to assuage feelings of loss, guilt and anger' (Hudson and Ineichen, 1991: p47).

Good and timely counselling support is essential:

When abortion is chosen under pressure or in haste, the likelihood of negative outcomes is increased. For some, the process is akin to one of mourning, in which the natural stages of grief and loss must be worked through. The teenager who chooses to terminate her pregnancy needs to feel that the decision is the right one for her.

Moore and Rosenthal, 1993: p153.

To choose an abortion needs intellectual and emotional maturity which is not usual in the younger mothers. Hudson and Ineichen suggest that girls' attitudes towards pregnancy and abortion develop according to their maturity and stage of adolescence. They found the following:

- *Early adolescence:* A girl may have only a hazy awareness of contraception and may deny her pregnancy and the responsibility for it. She cannot see herself as a mother or the foetus as a live baby. Thus she may accept an abortion for herself (although she may not condone it in others).
- *Middle adolescence:* A girl is more likely to be aware of contraception and take responsibility for her own behaviour. However responsibility for pregnancy may still be evaded. If abortion is accepted she may blame it on her boyfriend, parents, doctors or others.
- *Late adolescence:* A girl is likely to know what she is doing and take responsibility for the pregnancy. She is more likely to feel right about the decision she takes, including abortion, and not suffer disturbing after-effects.

Abridged from Hudson and Ineichen, 1991: p47.

Hudson and Ineichen suggest that middle class girls are more likely to opt for abortion than their more socio-economically deprived peers.

Providing support

The first part of this chapter gives insight into just some of the issues involved when providing support for a pregnant teenager. However, before plunging in to help, the helper needs to be aware of their own beliefs and prejudices. As the vulnerable young woman has decisions to make or reappraise, she can be easily influenced by someone she already respects and trusts. Each one of us has our own personal views: pro or anti-abortion, pro or anti-adoption etc. We might be so confident about our own stance and be so sure that it is 'right' (moral, ethical) that we may not realise that it is not the 'right' decision for the future of the young woman who has come for help. We may feel that we can judge what is right for a particular woman…but time may prove us wrong.

The contrasting case studies on page 110 demonstrate that while a young woman may seem set on a particular decision, all options and their future consequences may not truly have been considered.

Listening and providing a stepping-stone

The long-term consequences of any decision made by a pregnant girl are obviously so far-reaching that any outsider presuming to give advice (however well-meaning) should be fully aware of having a position of influence. Allen and Bourke Dowling (1998) found that a woman will consult very few people and is likely to look for people who will back her tentative decision. She may see those who offer other perspectives as 'unsympathetic'. However, it may be necessary

Maya and her baby

Maya was a quiet 16 year old from a religious family where abortion was not to be contemplated. She was naïve and had not realised that her boyfriend would somehow inveigle her into 'going further than was decent'. Afterwards she did not want to see him again. Pregnancy was a real shock. The few women in whom she confided all respected her religious background and judged that she would get family support with the baby.

Maya had romantic ideas about having a baby but when he was born she found him demanding and tiring. He was also a painful reminder of shattered dreams that she could not now fulfil. As he grew older she left him to her already over-worked mother. Maya often wished that he had never been born.

Toni's termination

15 year old Toni was academically bright and confident. She and Bud, her long-term boyfriend had been using condoms but, on the one occasion they did not have one, they decided to risk it. 'Unluckily,' she got pregnant. She confided in her disappointed parents. They were strongly in favour of an abortion. If she had a baby all her plans to go to university would be spoilt. She would just need to get it over, put it behind her and get on with her life. Her boyfriend was ambivalent but his parents were also sure that the pair should not be parents and jeopardise their futures.

The counsellor at the clinic, meeting a confident and articulate young couple, assessed that the woman had arrived at a considered decision and did not spend long going back over all the pros and cons.

Toni had the abortion at 11 weeks but it was not all over. She had counselling support but she still felt angry with her parents, with Bud and his parents and most of all with herself. How could she have agreed? She just could not concentrate on her studies.

She did not allow herself to take the examinations the following summer as she 'should have been looking after her baby.' She was convinced that she was an organised enough person who, with supportive parents on a reasonable income, could have managed to care for a baby and eventually attend the local university on a part-time basis. She had heard of other girls who had done just that.

to fall out of favour. Gently introducing the idea of other options may nudge the woman into further considering her decision and to being receptive to meeting a professional who has the training and skill to discuss the decision more fully.

- Listen to the young woman without interrupting.
  Keep your body language controlled as you remain empathetic and concerned. Your reactions will determine whether she will be receptive to what you have to say.
- Prompts:
  - Has she told her partner, her parents...?
  - Their reactions?
  If she has not yet told her parents or guardians you may need to discuss who and how she will tell, particularly if she is under 16. It may be possible to talk through best approaches and likely reactions.
- What does she think her options are?
  If at this stage she does not know and would like help from a professional, this is a good time to help her to make an appointment for the local advisory centre or clinic.

  Be aware: *Although all clinics and centres say that they give unbiased counselling, journalists have shown that various charitable institutions may not do so (Donnellan, 1997.) Before referral, check out an agency with your supervisor or colleagues.*

  If referral to someone else is unwelcome (her mind is already made up, she can't face telling anyone else...).
- Explain that for the moment you are going to take a neutral stand and point out all three options, including those she has already mentioned.
- Find out what she knows about each.
- If you are sufficiently informed, expand on the ones she knows little about saying that you are not an expert – but that other professionals can explain much more. Finding out more may not cause her to change her mind, but she will know that she is making her decision based on knowledge.
- The decision must be her own. Others may seek to influence her – but she has to think what will be right for her.
- Again suggest that you can help her make an appointment, refer etc.
- Explain that if she is not happy after she has seen that person or been to that agency there are still other options – but to remember that if she delays that she is actually making a decision by doing nothing.
- If you are in a position to be able to give more support over time – whatever she decides to do – then say so.
  She may need more time before seeing someone else. Remain available if possible:
- Suggest a time for another meeting – in about a week's time.

  A woman may ask what you would do in her position. Do not allow yourself to be in the position of making the decision. You can only get her to explore all the consequences of the different options. The decision must be hers.

Contact:

Brook Advisory Centres – for free and confidential advice to young people under 25. **Tel: 0800 0185 023. Website: http://www.brook.org.uk/**

Post-termination support

Most clinics offer counselling support for a few weeks after terminations. However a young woman may turn to her mentor for support. Listening and allowing the young woman to mourn and grieve may be sufficient but if, over time, she is functioning poorly in everyday life then she should be referred to her counsellor or her GP. This is an issue for discussion with one's supervisor.

Teenage mothers

Teenage mothers are as individual as other adolescents. Some manage quite well, caring for their babies and continuing their own lives, while others barely cope. Some are still striving to face the challenges of their own adolescence (completing an education and gaining qualifications or working with a view to becoming financially independent), while others have given up on their own development and are resigned to dependency. For most motherhood in reality is not as rosy, cosy or romantic as it seemed to be during pregnancy.

This book does not intend to cover the different ways of supporting teenage mothers and their babies as there are programmes and agencies which can give specialist advice and support. Health visitors are usually knowledgeable about local support. The youth worker or mentor may find information about groups, some of which will encourage the mother's own development and others which will help her to develop her relationship with her baby and stimulate its development.

Helpful organisations

Home-Start – Organisation with volunteer support for mothers with young children – see website page for 'health professionals' and for local schemes.
http://www.home-start.org.uk/

Sure Start – Government initiative for programmes to help babies and children (particularly the disadvantaged), to flourish at home and to prepare to get the most out of school.
http://www.surestart.gov.uk/

Occasional support

Just like older mothers, even the most organised young mother who appears to have a good support network and be coping well may have periods of feeling overwhelmed and at a loss. The mentor whose work with the teenage mother is focused on education or job training may occasionally find discussion ranging over other concerns.

Yasmin's case study illustrates that support may be needed unexpectedly. It is helpful if the mother can be helped to identify the person most likely to be able to provide appropriate support. By asking for herself she can feel in control and she is more likely to accept advice than if it is thrust upon her.

Case study: 'I may not be a fit mother'

19 year old Yasmin was looking increasingly depressed. Married very young and living with her in-laws, she was a full-time mother to her two year old son. Her husband and his parents were supportive, but they spent seven days a week in the family business while Yasmin and her sister-in-law looked after the house and the children.

Yasmin sometimes chatted to the tutor when she took her husband's youngest sister for a lesson. Over a cup of tea Yasmin let her 'happy mask' slip. She felt guilty because when she was very tired she was short-tempered with her little boy. He was so naughty compared with her sister-in-law's two beautifully behaved girls. When the family did get together, he always played up and she found herself treating him quite harshly. Afterwards she might slap him. She was worried about her own reactions but she did not seem to be able to stop herself. She did not dare tell her husband and if anyone else found out they would take the baby away for she obviously was such a bad mother.

The tutor could hear some alarm bells ringing but she also kept her sense of perspective. Yasmin was a sensible young woman who needed support. Talking about Yasmin's relationship with her mother-in-law and sister-in-law revealed an uneasy situation. Yasmin felt insecure and feared losing her beloved child. The tutor asked whether there was anyone who knew that Yasmin was a good mother. Yasmin was scared of her health visitor, but there was a nurse at the baby clinic where she used to attend regularly. The nurse had been positive and supportive about early problems. The tutor suggested that Yasmin return to the clinic with her son to talk to that nurse, or failing that another nurse or the doctor. The tutor stressed again that she was a good mother, who had recognised some danger signs and was asking for help. Yasmin must now get help for herself and her child as soon as possible. By the following week she should return to the tutor and let her know whom she had told.

The following week Yasmin arrived looking much calmer and less depressed. She had found another really helpful health visitor at the clinic who had already introduced her to a mother and toddler group. She would give her permission for the tutor to contact the health visitor.

(The tutor was pleased and relieved. Had Yasmin not found herself help, she would have taken a more active role to ensure that the two-year old was not in danger from an overwrought and depressed mother.)

Difficult young mothers

Some young women feel victimised for they have been continually let down by others. The boyfriend who was dead set against her having an abortion and who promised to support her may have lost interest or found a new relationship. Her family may be less supportive than she had anticipated, particularly if they are all living together in cramped conditions. So by the time she meets the housing officer who has little to offer she reacts badly. In fact she may react aggressively towards everyone in what she sees as a fight to get somewhere acceptable to live, adequate financial support and basic healthcare for herself and her child. In such circumstances anyone who really wants to help must be patient and under-standing of her insecurity and immaturity. Though unacceptable behaviour cannot be tolerated, the door to future meetings should be left open. Hopefully she will learn to modify her behaviour and her manners because she will realise that that is the only way forward towards her goal. Though the young mother may be seeking practical help, often the counselling which she receives along the way may be equally valuable. (Hudson and Ineichen, 1991).

Teenage fathers

While teenage mothers receive a great deal of support, teenage fathers may be ignored. In fact fathers below the age of 20 make up about 30 per cent of the partners to teenage mothers (Allen and Bourke Dowling, 1998). However, although it is recognised that children with involved and supportive fathers fare better than those with absent or non-involved fathers (Jaffee et al., 2001) in the UK there is little support available for young fathers.

In the United States there are schemes to support teenage fathers (Kiselica, 1990). They recognise that on hearing about the pregnancy a young father may face a variety of emotional reactions including depression, anger or denial of responsibility. They may then have to deal with:

- Decision-making, e.g. adoption or abortion.
- Conflicts with the mother and her family.
- Conflict regarding access to the child.
- Concern over competency in parenting.

Over the longer term the father who decides to give support may have personal concerns about:

- Dropping out of education.
- Legal concerns.
- Long-term commitment.
- Possible marriage.
- Employment worries.
- Financial hardship.
- Changing relationships with his peers.
- Long-term career dissatisfaction.

Kiselica (1990) reports that many of the fathers who attend schemes, with oppor-tunity to explore all the issues listed above and their role as a father, do tend to support the mothers both emotionally and financially, continuing throughout the child's early years.

A youth worker or mentor initially offering support to a young man may find him unwilling or unable to discuss his feelings. Establishing a relationship may best be accomplished alongside practical help. This may involve helping him to find employment, giving him information that he can share with his partner or showing him how to access legal advice. If he is to have regular contact with the baby, then he will need some practical childcare skills too. In time he may be able to discuss the emotions affecting him and the decisions to be made and those already taken. While the young father may need help from professionals to sort out legal or financial implications, ongoing emotional support and just having someone to listen can be of great value.

Ideally there should be parenting classes for fathers as well as mothers but...

Not exacerbating problems for mother and child

A note of caution must be sounded before suggesting wholehearted encouragement for teenage fathers playing a full role in their children's lives. Jaffee et al. (2001) investigated a group of teenage fathers taken from a cohort of over 1,000 children in New Zealand followed from their birth in 1972–73. The likelihood of becoming a young father was associated with having a history of conduct disorder, criminal convictions, low socio-economic status, living with a single parent and having poor quality relationships with their parents. While within the sample there were some excellent fathers fully involved with their children, they also found that those fathers who were absent from their children's lives were more likely to exhibit criminal behaviour, drug use, unemployment and low educational attainment. Since other studies have shown that these traits are associated with poor parenting, they warn that encouraging such fathers to get more involved with their children may not be in the best interests of the children unless the fathers are given a substantial amount of help. Such men have to meet their own challenges in the transition to adulthood before they can become supportive partners and fathers. Without the right sort of ongoing support, immature and inadequate fathers could make a difficult situation even worse.

To round up

The research studies all seem to reach the same general conclusions. Interventions should aim to prevent teenage pregnancy. While there are some examples of good teenage parenting, delaying parenthood for greater maturity is definitely preferable. Where teenagers do become parents, both mothers and fathers require good ongoing and regular support.

Chapter 14

Overwhelming Emotions: Stress, Depression, Suicidal Thoughts, Self-injury and Eating Disorders

Previous chapters have discussed some of the different circumstances and experiences that cause distress to a young person and may lead to maladaptive behaviour. This chapter explains some of the causes, signs and symptoms of stress, depression, despair, self-injury, suicidal thinking and eating disorders in adolescents. Ways to respond to each of them are suggested.

Although mental health conditions are described under different headings for clarity, the reader should understand that an individual may suffer from more than one condition and clinical diagnosis may not always be clear-cut.

Adolescence is a time of development and adjustment. Adjustment requires change and change creates emotive reactions, some of which are experienced negatively as anxiety and stress. Thus negotiating adolescence, even in the absence of serious problems, can be stressful. Anyone working with adolescents is bound to encounter their different ways of managing or not managing their stress. Sometimes a youth worker is confronted by a crisis and needs to provide immediate support. Occasionally a youth worker may be the first to recognise that a young person is not coping in their everyday life or is in danger of self-harm and needs support from a mental health professional.

Individuals deal differently with stress and they have different levels of resilience. Some know that even after the most dreadful experiences, life can go on and some happiness can be found again. Others cannot envisage survival. Some will react angrily to the smallest amounts of frustration or discomfort, while others will bear a mounting load of disappointments and provocation until a final act will 'blow their fuse'. While some will display their feelings, shout or hit out at others, other individuals will turn in on themselves blaming themselves, turning to alcohol or drugs or even physically injuring themselves. It is obviously easier to recognise those acting out than those turning inwards.

There are gender differences too. While many females are able to talk about their problems and their feelings, males may be less able or willing to do so. Young women are more likely to self-harm and may talk about and attempt suicide, but more young men succeed in committing suicide.

Stress and anxiety

We all need a certain amount of stress to kick us into action. For example, exams are a regular feature in the lives of most teenagers but unless there is some pressure to succeed and some anxiety about failure or not doing well enough, there is no impetus to put in any work or effort beforehand. A little anxiety about important exams or interviews will create enough tension and stress for the student to prepare and perform to the best of their ability. However, too much anxiety and an overload of stress will overwhelm, with the result that the student will be unable to concentrate, or even be physically sick or unable to get out of bed on the morning of the exam.

It may help an adolescent to be able to recognise the physical signs of stress in themselves. Some will recall these physiological reactions of 'preparing for flight' from their biology lessons but may not actually relate what they have learned to what they experience when things go wrong.

Physical signs of stress may include:

- quickening heart rate
- shallow, rapid breathing
- dry mouth
- sweating
- trembling
- tightening in the pit of the stomach
- inability to eat or increased need to eat

The body is tensing and preparing to run away from physical danger (e.g. escaping from a ferocious dog) with blood going from the abdomen to the legs to boost the running. Once we have escaped, the body can relax again and the symptoms will subside.

However, unlike running from physical danger, we cannot usually escape from difficult emotional or social situations. The body might continue to react physiologically and then overreact, leading to some of the following:

- inability to stay still e.g. pacing the floor, hand-wringing, fidgeting
- feelings of nausea
- vomiting or diarrhoea
- hyper-ventilation – difficulty breathing (breathing out too much carbon dioxide and building up too much oxygen in the blood)
- feeling faint (blood is drained away from the head)

Some of these symptoms might constitute what is known as a 'panic attack.'

Immediate treatment

Fainting: help the patient to sit down, loosen tight clothing and help lower head between knees – or lie down with raised legs – so that blood can return to head. Relax. When rested raise to sitting position slowly. Give sips of water.

Hyperventilating: get more carbon dioxide into the blood by breathing in what is being breathed out. This can be done by the patient cupping their hands over their mouth to make a mask, exhale and then inhale. Even better is to breathe into a paper (not plastic) bag and inhale. Continue doing this for a few minutes. Then encourage the patient to relax, particularly around the stomach, and start breathing normally again taking full breaths. Treat for shock.

In either case, afterwards keep the patient relaxed. Do not start talking about the bad news or the worrying thoughts that triggered the attack because this could trigger another attack. Instead try to divert attention away from the concerns and also away from the body so that it can relax and return to normal.

Anticipating stress reaction and using counselling skills

Anticipation or quick thinking may prevent the stress symptoms from building into a full panic attack or faint. After bad news, a shock or a series of frustrations an individual may turn pale, tremble, sweat or breathe shallow breaths:

- Calmly and gently help them to a seat.
- Suggest that they release any tight clothing, especially top buttons and belts or waistbands.
- Encourage physical relaxation. 'Just let your shoulders drop and let your stomach muscles relax.'
- 'Take slow deep breaths.' 'Put your hand on the lower part of your chest and feel your lungs breathe in and out.'
- You will be able to monitor their recovery by colour returning to cheeks or deeper breathing, reduced trembling etc.
- Divert them from thinking about original concerns until they have fully recovered.

Once fully recovered it may be appropriate to suggest they go home with the offer of talking things through in a few days. Make contact a little later to demonstrate that you are concerned and also to fix a time to meet, if the young person wishes.

If the young person remains in your care, you should give them time to recover. Explain that there will be time to talk if they wish but do not set a time as this might cause further stress.

Talking about dealing with stress

In the subsequent meeting talk through the issues using the usual counselling skills protocol. If this was a one-off situation (such as receiving bad news) and the panic situation is not later mentioned by the young person, it does not need to be addressed. However, if it is a situation likely to arise again, such as taking examinations, attending important meetings or court appearances, then the adolescent should be encouraged to talk the situation through. If they are concerned that it can happen again then they should be encouraged or helped to make an appointment with their GP or a counsellor. Put it into context:

- Explain that these are physiological processes.
- They have identified that they react in a certain way in particular situations.
- They are taking control and therefore being strong (not weak) by requesting professional help so that they can manage themselves better in such situations in the future.
- A health professional will be able to suggest some techniques or exercises which help to control the physiological reactions.
- Use discretion when mentioning 'psychologists' or 'counsellors' because some young people will worry about being seen as 'mad' or 'weak' and will feel even worse or resist getting help.

There are some good self-help books aimed at teenagers and to be found in local libraries.

Suggested reading

Haughton, E. (1995) *Dealing With STRESS*. Hove: Wayland.
Scott-Cameron, N. (2000) *Bad Hair Day? A Guide to Dealing with Everyday Stress*. Shaftesbury: Element.

Depression

Failing to cope with the challenges and stresses of adolescence may cause depression in a young person. However Caldwell (1999) suggests that the symptoms of depression may be difficult to recognise because they include the changes in behaviour which are expected in adolescence:

- slow responses
- sullenness
- flatness in affect/mood and speech
- tenseness, fidgeting and irritability
- social withdrawal
- mood swings
- changes in weight
- changes in sleep patterns
- tendency to 'catastrophise' – making minor events into major crises

We all get depressed at times and particularly in reaction to difficult life events such as bereavement, failure, changes, illness and injury. This is normal and it signals to others that we need care, sympathy and consideration. It can be likened to the passive behaviour of 'animals, whose crawling or cowering away may be a sign of submission to ward off aggressive attacks' (Wright, 1997: p112). However when this behaviour persists unabated over a long period an adolescent may be retreating into a depressive illness, which is a way of escaping from a lifestyle that has become too difficult to bear.

Geldard and Geldard (1999) discuss depression as exhibited by adolescents. *Dysthymia* is a mild but persistent form of depression, which may include the symptoms mentioned above and some of the following:

- Loss of interest and energy.
- Poor concentration and memory.
- Feelings of inadequacy.
- Low self-esteem.
- Feelings of guilt, anger, hopelessness and despair.

Following The World Health Organisation definitions they give guidance for recognising the level of depression:

- **Mild depression**: effort is required to carry out normal daily tasks.
- **Moderate depression**: everyday social and or working life is affected. The individual is prevented from doing some tasks that need to be done.
- **Severe depression**: there is a marked effect on everyday life. There may be psychotic symptoms such as hallucinations or delusions.

Depression may be caused by long-term problems, by a serious loss or by a series of loss experiences:

- History of parental divorce or separation.
- Death of a loved one: family member, a friend or a pet.
- Inability to escape punishment (e.g. bullying, abuse).
- Separation from long-term friends (e.g. after moving house).
- Receiving a low level of positive reinforcement (never being praised or feeling appreciated).

There is a gender difference (Caldwell, 1999; Geldard and Geldard, 1999). Girls are more likely to turn inwards, thinking negatively about themselves and their environments and so becoming depressed, while boys are more likely to react by acting out aggressively. However some young men do suffer from depression and they need to be identified and given support too (Caldwell, 1999).

The depressed adolescent may feel unable to control themselves and unable to influence anything in the world around them. If this becomes a downward spiral, they need help. The task of the initial supporter is to indicate that they value the young person and, with their permission, will be willing to help. The first stage is to enable a trusting relationship to develop. After experiencing a relationship in which they feel safe and supported, they may be able to assume sufficient control and the courage to take up referral to a counsellor or therapist with whom they can form a new relationship and begin the therapeutic work to bring about change.

Using counselling skills

- Use the approach discussed in Chapter 3, demonstrating the key qualities.
- Explain that you are not a counsellor but that you do have some knowledge that may be helpful.
- Explain honestly about confidentiality and explain who you might have to inform.
- If the young person is willing to talk, then listen.
- Often the young person does not know what to say and does not know what is expected in this strange one-to-one situation.
- Explain that it might be helpful to talk about what help would be available.
- You may mention a couple of the symptoms that you have observed 'You have been rather quiet…you seem a bit tired….' and encourage them to talk about other symptoms. You can prompt with questions about appetite and sleep. This may encourage talk about feelings.
- Ask the length of time they have been experiencing these feelings.
- Try, if possible, to avoid delving into the history of the depression or its causes in depth. (This is the counsellor's territory and again you do not want to unpack too much.)
- Obviously if your warmth and caring attitude has unlocked feelings and the story starts to tumble out, listen, without interrupting.
- Respond genuinely, containing any shock you may feel.
- Acknowledge that it has been courageous/trusting to be able to speak about this.
- Now that they have been able to tell you, together you can find a way of getting appropriate help. Parental circumstances and permission may have to be considered.
- They may naturally be reluctant or resistant. Preparing for referral may be slow.
- Using your common sense you may be able to suggest some interim measures to improve the present situation – but don't offer this as a simple fix (it is only a temporary sticking plaster).
- If you have not had time to prepare, you may want to give yourself time to think about appropriate referral and to consult your supervisor.
- If the young person has been depressed for a while, then taking time will allow them to prepare too.
- Suggest that you meet again the following week to start thinking how you can proceed together. You will be giving ongoing support until a referral is successfully taken up.
- The process above may be slow and it may take a few meetings over a few weeks for a relationship to be established at all and then more for any meaningful dialogue. Don't be alarmed by silence or by tears. Just sit through them patiently.
- Depression and a sense of hopelessness significantly increase the likelihood of suicide. **If there is any talk of suicide – take this seriously** (see below).

Suicide

The Samaritans (2002) report that suicide accounts for over a fifth of all deaths of young people, with at least two suicides each day by people under the age of 25 in the UK and Republic of Ireland. Eighty per cent of suicides are committed by young men (approximately 17 per 100,000 men between the ages of 15 and 24). Alcohol and substance abuse are a significant factor in these youth suicides, probably because alcohol and drugs act as depressants and can affect thinking and reasoning.

Attempted suicide is also a major health problem among young people with their rates being much higher than the rest of the population. Most attempts are made by young women, but men are more likely to succeed (The Samaritans, cited in Donnellan, 2000). In addition young Asian women in the UK whose families originate from the Indian sub-continent are at greater risk of suicide and attempted suicide than their non-Asian peers. They cite cultural conflict and difficulties with parents, families and marital partners as the source of their problems (The Samaritans, ibid.).

Reasons for suicidal thoughts and actions

A great deal of research has been focused on adolescents who have suicidal thoughts and those who attempt and commit suicide. Studies have investigated family and social backgrounds, psychological profiles and precipitating events. This book can give only brief facts and pointers, up-to-date and detailed help can be obtained on the Internet. (See end of section.)

These adolescents frequently come from *families with severe difficulties*. Robbins (1998) reports that they are more likely than their peers to have a parent suffering from psychiatric illness, or problems of alcohol or substance abuse, or a history of suicide attempts. They tend to report a high level of conflict with their parents and feel that they do not receive support from their families. Girls who had attempted suicide were more likely than others to have histories of physical or sexual abuse or neglect in childhood.

Robbins (1998) summarises the *psychological profile* of an adolescent with suicidal thoughts and at risk of taking suicidal action as having many of the following characteristics:

- Signs of depression.
- Expressions of hopelessness that things will never get better.
- Way of looking at unpleasant events and turning them into catastrophes.
- Low self-esteem.
- Impulsiveness.
- High level of anger – often directed towards self.
- Perfectionist standards.
- Ineffective coping techniques.

The precipitating event may be just one significant event or a series of things going wrong with a final incident which 'breaks the camel's back'. Different studies (Robbins, 1998; The Samaritans, cited in Donnellan, 2000) concur that these significant experiences may include:

- Recent loss (e.g. parent, sibling, close friend, pet).
- Break up of a close relationship.
- Major disappointment (e.g. exam failure).
- Change of circumstances (e.g. loss of job, loss of status, imprisonment, loss of home).
- Major conflict within the family or at school (e.g. bullying incident).

The young person who is already coping poorly and has over-invested in a particular relationship for support may reach the point of despair. They cannot see the situation as ever improving and they feel out of control. If their way of responding is by acting rather than talking, then they may just react impulsively and choose death as the only way out.

Alternatively they may turn to alcohol or drugs which will cloud their judgement and increase the likelihood of suicide or accidental death.

Warning signs

It is a myth that people who talk about committing suicide don't carry it through. Some do. The warning signs that a young person may be thinking about suicide may include:

- Saying that there is no sign of hope or that there is no point to life.
- Talking of suicide 'I wish I was dead!' 'I'm going to end it all!'
- Risk-taking or careless behaviour.
- Sudden striking mood change or signs of mental disturbance (e.g. hallucinations).
- Giving away treasured or personal possessions.
- Seeming unnaturally cheerful after a period of despondency.
- Withdrawal or apathy.

However warning signs are not always so obvious. Studies have shown that people visit their GP in the week before committing suicide but do not talk about their suicidal thoughts or intentions.

Interventions and support

Whether an individual is thinking about suicide or is acting in a suicidal manner, the most important support is to be there with them, giving time, patience, understanding and attention:

- Ask them about their thoughts and whether they were thinking of suicide. Don't avoid it. Talking about suicide will not be putting the idea into their head. They may be relieved to talk.

- Listen – keeping the key qualities in mind – treating them with respect etc. and not being judgmental.
- Take them seriously and try to understand their perspective.
- Show that you care by the way you act – as you may not need to say much.
- Give reassurance that desperate feelings are common but that people find that situations can and do change for the better.
- Offer practical support. Try and find something that will help alleviate the immediate situation – but do not promise something you cannot deliver. (Do not promise confidentiality or availability that you cannot manage.)
- Try to work out together with the young person what the next step should be (e.g. referral, going to stay with someone) so that they will feel safe.
- Tell someone else so that you do not have sole responsibility.
- If you are genuinely concerned about another suicide attempt, err on the side of safety and immediately inform any professional who has had contact with the individual. Do not leave them alone.

Do not make them feel worse by:
- Lecturing or criticising them or telling them it was 'a silly thing to do'.
- Pretending it has not happened – or changing the subject.
- Rejecting them or leaving them alone.
- Asking loads of questions or talking too much yourself.
- Minimising the problems.
- Hurrying them.

A little later:
- In the longer term help them to find a counsellor, or other professional support or good informal support.
- Give information about telephone helplines – for times like the middle of the night.
- Suggest a GP appointment because monitoring or medical intervention may be appropriate.
- Keep contact and try to promote social contact with other young people.

After an overdose

Ross (2002a) gives the following advice:

> A small overdose of **paracetamol** can kill. If a person has taken paracetamol, **take them to hospital**, even if they have vomited and are feeling better. Pumping out the stomach within a couple of hours of an overdose, followed by medication can protect the liver if it is given soon enough (approximately within 24 hours). **Liver damage** is maximal 3–4 days after an overdose and is a common cause of **death**.

> After an overdose a young person may lie about what they have taken. Do not trust them. Take them to hospital for assessment. A blood or urine test may reveal something which can be treated and save life.

After a suicide attempt

Most of those who are saved from their suicide attempts are eventually grateful. Ross (2002 a) reports that most students who have taken overdoses intending to kill themselves and have then been treated in hospital and given support, have been grateful. Even though they may have resisted treatment at the time, they have eventually changed from their pessimistic view that life was hopeless, etc.

However some people do try to commit suicide again – and they succeed.

After suicide

Suicide cannot always be prevented. Those left behind may feel responsible and guilty that they did not recognise the situation or do more to help. These feelings together with many unanswered questions may aggravate all the usual emotions of loss associated with bereavement. Professional support may be recommended (see Chapter 15).

The youth worker or mentor who has been involved with a young person who has attempted or committed suicide must also allow time for themselves. Good support, with plenty of time to think and to talk, and good supervision are essential.

Useful contacts

Childline – Helpline for young people – Free phone 0800 1111

The Samaritans – 24 hour Helpline – 0345 909090

Self-injury

Deliberate self-injury among adolescents is more prevalent than a lay person might suspect. The Samaritans (2002) quote research data from the Centre for Suicide Research at Warne Hospital, Oxford that in the UK an estimated 24,000 young people self-harmed during 1998, which was equivalent to three every hour. Women who self-injure significantly outnumber men with an estimated female:male ratio of 7:1 (Royal College of Psychiatrists, cited in Donnellan, 2000).

Ross (2002b) defines self-injury as the deliberate infliction of pain or injury to one's own body which stops short of suicidal intent. Cutting arms or legs is the most frequent form of self-harm. Other forms include burning and scalding oneself, scratching or biting and also pulling out hair or eyelashes. Taking a drugs overdose is also self-harm. Some individuals use more than one form, depending on their feelings. Usually self-injury takes place in private and in secret. The young person is aware that parents, friends or others would be upset and try to stop them if they knew about it. Sometimes even when regularly seeing a counsellor or a GP an individual may still not mention their self cutting.

Reasons for self-injury

Self-injury is another way of dealing with emotional distress and feelings, such as shame, anger and self-loathing. The emotional pain is turned towards the self and experienced as physical pain. Some individuals talk about releasing a 'tension' when they experience the pain; those with unbearable feelings of guilt or shame may be punishing themselves. Some feel emotionally dead or numb and feel that by inflicting injury they are gaining control because the pain makes them feel more alive (Donnellan, 2000; Ross, 2002b).

The sort of distress which leads to self-injury can be much the same as those precursors to depression or suicide mentioned above. This behaviour can be an increasing response to childhood trauma or mistreatment (abuse or neglect), family difficulties or more recent trauma or serious problems.

In recent years increasing rates of self-harm have been reported among young lesbians and gay men. Ross suggests that this may be a response to internal emotional turmoil and distress as they formulate their sexuality and also a reaction to external discrimination or abuse.

Needing help

> Anyone who is harming themselves is struggling to cope and needs help. If people don't get help when they need it, problems are likely to continue. Problems may also get a lot worse and the effects may 'snowball'. Some people will continue to harm themselves more and more seriously. They may even end up killing themselves.
>
> Royal College of Psychiatrists, 2000, cited in Donnellan, 2000: p7.

Youth workers should also bear in mind that 'copy-cat' behaviour can occur in a small group of peers with problems (see Chapter 8). Again this may have fatal consequences (Royal College of Psychiatrists, Ibid).

Helpful interventions

Once again the youth worker should aim to get the young person to seek professional help. The process may be slow (taking more than one meeting) and meet with resistance:

- Whatever your own feelings of shock, upset, anger, fear, repugnance, etc., keep them well hidden. You may be the first person they have ever told or shown and your reaction may determine whether they dare to go any further in getting help. Do not do or say anything which could be construed as disapproval or blame or indicate your disappointment.
- Keep the key qualities in mind; listen and be willing to hear even unpleasant details of injuries if necessary.
- Admitting the self-injury is the first step to recovery. If the person has told you, then they have made a tentative move towards trying to stop. They have taken some control and have been courageous. Acknowledge this.
- Keep your mind on the person, not the injury.
- Don't compromise yourself by promising confidentiality. By telling you – or allowing you to find out – they have indicated that they really wanted someone to know. They may accidentally kill themselves. (Consult your supervisor or a colleague – don't keep this to yourself.)

- Explain that the health services will have come across this before and have different ways to help the individual to:
  - Minimise the risks.
  - Gain control over the urge to self-injure.
  - Understand why it happens.
  - Recognise situations which trigger the urge.
  - Anticipate and avoid some risky situations.
- Suggest some ways of keeping safe when the urges are strong:
  - If cutting: avoid major arteries, veins and organs.
  - Keep to hand a first aid kit and access to a phone with numbers of supportive friends and GP.
  - Avoid alcohol and non-prescription drugs because they can impair judgement and result in more harm than intended.
- Try to develop some diversions for when the urges feel very strong such as:
  - Keeping hands and brain busy: cooking, doing puzzles, Internet surfing.
  - Call a friend.
  - Go to a public place where you wouldn't harm yourself.
  - Give yourself another less harmful sensory experience, such as putting an elastic band around the wrist and twanging it or holding an ice cube.
  - Go out and do physical exercise.
  - Draw red crayon over the limbs instead of cutting to draw blood.

*These interim suggestions should only be used if there is no immediate prospect of the young person getting professional help. Do **not** take on the role of substitute counsellor.*

Above all – remain in contact with the young person. Continue the relationship, offering support and encouraging them to take up professional help.

Suggestions for this protocol have been adapted from Ross, 2002b.

Useful websites

www.selfinjury.freeserve.co.uk

Mental Health Foundation: www.mentalhealth.org.uk

Eating disorders: Anorexia and Bulimia

Eating disorders are included in this chapter because they too may result from ways of attempting to cope with emotional distress. Again there is a gender difference; these disorders are more common among females than males. They may begin with a little dieting but then the dieting escalates into an obsession and food and body weight take on enormous significance in life, affecting both psychological and physical health.

Anorexic and bulimic behaviour tends to take hold during the ages of 15–20 but children as young as 10 or 11 years old may recognise that they have an eating problem and ask for help (Childline, 1996, cited in Donnellan, 1998b). Although up to 10 per cent of teenage girls may have a very mild form of eating disorder (over-concern with dieting), it is estimated that about 1 per cent of adolescent girls have true anorexia or bulimia. These eating disorders are particularly common in families where academic and social achievements are highly valued, but they do occur in all sections of the community (Eating Disorders Association, 1998, cited in Donnellan, 1998b).

Anorexia nervosa can be recognised in unhealthy weight loss and a preoccupation with weight leading to food avoidance. The Eating Disorders Association describes the common symptoms as:

- Intense concern or fear about gaining weight.
- Voluntary starvation leading to weight loss.
- Rigid control of diet and lifestyle.
- Cessation of menstruation.
- Excessive exercise routine.
- Cold hands and feet.
- Dry skin.
- Hair loss.
- Overwhelming feelings of guilt or self-loathing.
- Depression.
- Obsession with food.
- Perfectionism.
- Withdrawal or secrecy.
- Fatigue.

If the problem gets out of hand and body weight falls below a critical level, death can result.

In Bulimia nervosa the individual eats excessive amounts of food, i.e. 'bingeing', and then purges themselves by starvation, vomiting, laxatives or diuretics. Life can revolve around buying food, preparing food, bingeing and then getting rid of it. The Eating Disorders Association describes the following symptoms:

- Binge eating followed by fasting, laxative abuse, vomiting, excessive exercise or other purging.
- Loss of tooth enamel.
- Broken blood vessels in the face.
- Darkened circles under eyes.
- Fainting spells.
- Irregular heartbeat.
- Stomach ache.
- Perfectionism.
- Low self-esteem and striving to please others.
- Self-critical thoughts after a binge.
- Obsession with food and body weight.

Giving support

As eating disorders, like other behaviours mentioned in this chapter, may be a way of trying to cope with emotional stress, so providing support requires a similar counselling approach. Again the emphasis is on listening, creating a trusting relationship and then encouraging the young person to take control for themselves by getting professional help:

- Listen and encourage the young person to talk.
- Be understanding.
- Do not criticise or condemn.
- Inform them about different phone helplines.
- Encourage them to tell their parents if they do not already know.
- Encourage them to take control and research different sorts of help (therapies, self-help groups, GP support) as a 'window-shopper'.
- Encourage meeting a counsellor or GP to find out more – without necessarily committing to a treatment.
- If a treatment is undertaken, praise co-operation and positive responses – but don't criticise 'slips'.
- Model good eating habits.
- Continue to support – even if your suggestions are rejected.
- Be patient – the anorexic needs to accept and like themselves – this can be a very slow process.

Do not:

- Apply any sort of pressure around eating.
- Do not act as an amateur dietician – leave it to the professionals.

Useful contacts

Eating Disorders Association
1st Floor
Wensum House
103 Prince of Wales Road
Norwich
Norfolk
NR1 1DW
01603 619090
Website: www.gurney.org.uk/eda

Chapter 15

Death, Bereavement and Other Loss

This chapter looks at ways of supporting young people who are bereaved. It suggests some approaches for making contact after a death and for encouraging peer support. A brief description of the 'healthy' grieving process is included. Although most young people are able to grieve naturally with the informal support of family and friends and then begin to adapt to life without the person who has died, some adolescents do need professional help. The indications for referral are given.

Young people frequently experience the death of someone close to them. Many adolescents suffer the loss of grandparents while others face the death of a parent, a sibling or a close friend. Whoever has died and whatever the circumstances the young person will find it easier if others acknowledge their loss rather than avoiding the subject. Most bereaved adolescents will benefit from the opportunity to talk about their feelings. The majority learn to cope and to adjust with informal support from friends and from adults whom they already know, including those outside the immediate family. The youth worker or mentor may both give support themselves and encourage shy or embarrassed peers to do the same.

Initial contact

A youth worker can demonstrate appropriate care and concern by promptly contacting a group member, when someone significant in their life has died. Whether the initial contact is by telephone, by note or in person will depend on the circumstances but actually taking time to talk or to be with the young person should be the aim. Although many people are shy about approaching a home where a family member has died, grieving families often appreciate visitors who care about them. If the youth worker senses that a visit or phone call might be viewed as intrusive, then they may send a note saying that they will be calling in or phoning in a few days time.

Making the initial contact can be the hardest part. The youth worker phoning or visiting and being answered by someone they do not know may begin by:

- Introducing themselves – and mentioning their organisation if appropriate.
- Saying that they are sorry to hear of the death and that they have come to see or are telephoning to talk to (young person's name).

- Asking whether the present time is convenient – and, if not, trying to establish a better time.

The worst that can happen is that the person answering the door or phone is dismissive or the young person does not wish to talk or be visited. Even then the response will usually be of the 'Thank you, but no thank you' variety. The youth worker must then accept that they have done their best and should not press further. Seldom will there be a really negative or rude response but it can happen, and then the rejected caller may have to retreat and take solace in the knowledge that they have acted in a responsible way, acceptable to most.

More usually the young person will be pleased that someone has troubled to make contact with *them*. Ideally the venue should be comfortable and relatively private, but that is often impossible. Whether on the phone, in their home, at the local café or at the group meeting place, the aim of the contact is to allow them to express their feelings about the death and their loss.

Helpful approaches

- Stick to a normal everyday conversational approach with which you are both usually comfortable.
- Keep the questions as few as possible – but just enough to encourage talking. If appropriate try questions such as:
  - Was this death unexpected?
  - Do you want to talk about what happened?
  - Do you want to tell me more?
  - How are you?

Apart from the last question, the above are all closed questions so that the bereaved teenager can answer 'no'. If they do not wish to talk, then their privacy must be respected. In the early days after the death they just may not be ready to talk about it – but they may be pleased of the company and want to talk of other things:

- If it is obvious that they really do not want the visit or call, then the youth worker should steer it to an end:
  You may prefer not to talk to me today and I understand that. If you find in a few days or a few weeks that you do want to talk, then this is how to get hold of me (phone number and availability).
  Remain open, friendly and non-judgmental as you go. Just occasionally your leaving makes it easier to talk and the conversation as you are leaving can be helpful in itself.
- Listening attentively is really helpful. You may not be required to say much – but just to indicate that you are listening.
- Allow time for repetition – bereaved people frequently repeat the circumstances of the death, needing to go over it many times.

- Allow space to experience the pain of grief…'It's alright to cry…'
- Allow feelings of guilt, hurt or anger to be expressed, without stifling them.
- Show that it is also alright to laugh and be normal.
- Allow time for silence and thinking.
- If the visit is taking place quite soon after the death it may be appropriate to ask about the funeral arrangements.
- If the family's culture is different from that of the youth worker it may be helpful to acknowledge that and to find out about any particular customs of mourning.
- Five or ten minutes before needing to leave: *We have been talking for a while and I can stay a little longer but in…minutes or so I shall have to go.*
- Establish whether another call would be welcome. *Would you like me to call again in (a few days…a week…)?* (Don't promise an exact time – as you may be prevented by other circumstances.)

Avoiding unhelpful approaches

- Do not say: 'I know how you feel. My father died…' (You do not know how **they** feel. Every individual will feel differently. However tempting, do not talk about your own bereavement. You are there to think about them.)
- Try to avoid platitudes: 'Time is a great healer…' This may make only **you** feel better…it is more helpful to sit with the pain.
- Do not say: 'You'll soon feel better'. It is more helpful to say that you *understand that they are feeling very sad and upset and that in feeling sad they are remembering…*
- Do not assume anything! (The teenager may have had a bad relationship with the person who died: what appears to be a merciful release from one perspective, may be abandonment from another.)
- Do not try to cheer them up or try to stifle tears because this is an opportunity to really grieve with someone else present to acknowledge the pain.
- If you have said that you will call again, do not let them down.

Encouraging peer support

In mainstream UK culture death is often excluded from everyday life and treated as a taboo subject. Some teenagers may never have attended a funeral or experienced the death of someone close to them. Consequently when a friend is bereaved they may not know how to respond. Sometimes a young person is so shocked to find that the parent of a good school-friend has died that they feel it would be more respectful to keep away! Even a good friend might misguidedly believe that by talking about a death they will upset their friend more and so doesn't mention it at all.

From the initial contact the youth worker will be able to gauge whether the bereaved teenager has plenty of friends who are rallying round or whether the support network is fairly thin with the young person having to support others but with no-one there for them. If the young person is already part of a youth group, sports team or educational group, other young group members may need some encouragement to make contact and visit.

Given a little push in the right direction adolescents are good at supporting one

---

Case study: Uma getting back to school

12 year old Uma's father died suddenly and unexpectedly of a heart attack. It was during the school summer holidays. Her guide leader, Polly, learned about the death because Uma was unable to attend a day's outing. A phone call to Uma's home indicated that visiting one afternoon would be welcomed.

Polly found the house full of visitors but she was able to talk for a few minutes to Uma's mother and then she found Uma with her older sisters and other young people. Uma was rather shy and said little but meanwhile Polly realised that all the young people were really there for the older sisters and that there was no-one of Uma's age. Polly asked Uma about the mourning customs and found that Uma would be staying at home and expecting visitors for several more days.

That evening Polly contacted some of the Guides with whom Uma was friendly at meetings to tell them of her father's death and to let them know that they could call in. One girl visited a couple of times with her mother. Another phoned Polly a couple of days later to say that she and a friend would like to visit but that they felt a bit 'strange' about it. With their parents' permission Polly talked to the girls about how they might feel in a similar situation and about the mourning custom's of Uma's family and then took them over to Uma's house. Polly was relieved but not really surprised to find that after just a few awkward minutes the girls began chatting and then giggling. When Polly had to go Uma was reluctant to let the girls leave and they promised to return.

After her own holiday break, Polly was pleased to see that Uma returned to Guide meetings at the start of the autumn term. She seemed to be readjusting. Only several months later, on meeting Uma's mother in the street, did Polly learn that Uma had been dreading the return to school more than anything else. Fortunately two of the Guides who had visited went to the same school and their support had been invaluable.

---

another and can be sensitive to each other's needs. Most young people will have no difficulty respecting cultural and religious rituals surrounding death and mourning which are different from their own, as long as they know what to expect and an appropriate dress code (such as not revealing too much flesh). The youth worker does not need to be an expert on different religious customs as they can rely on the family of the bereaved adolescent to explain. When finding out whether visiting by outsiders would be welcomed they should also check whether there are particular times to avoid, such as prayer-times and meal-times.

Ongoing support

However, the ongoing support for many months after the death is even more important than the initial contact. There tend to be many who will offer support in the early days of grief but then friends and family get used to the death and they expect the immediately bereaved to adjust and 'get on with it'. The grieving process is frequently much slower than is generally recognised and an adolescent who appears to have 'got over' a death may suddenly react with anger or grow depressed when reaching a birthday or anniversary or facing another unexpected event. Friends can then play an important role in absorbing the fresh wave of grief and listening again and acknowledging that the loss is still there. The youth worker may be a listener too, or their role may be to support the friends who may not understand why their friend is still so distressed when they were sure they were 'getting better'.

The grieving process

While supporting someone who has been bereaved it can be helpful to know a little about the psychology of grieving. Individuals often ask:

Am I normal if I feel…?
Shouldn't I be feeling…?

Each person will experience different feelings depending on their own personalities, the circumstances of the death, whether it was expected or sudden and on the relationship with the deceased. They may feel sad, lonely, numb, angry, anxious, guilty, tired, relieved…the list is lengthy.

Murray-Parkes (1993) explains:

> *Grief is essentially an emotion that draws us towards something or someone that is missing. It arises from an awareness of a discrepancy between the world that is and the world that 'should be'.*
>
> Murray-Parkes, 1993: p242.

For example the adolescent grieving for a grandmother who lived in the family home may wake up in a morning some weeks after her death and experience emptiness. She feels sad but also full of self-reproach because sometimes she used to resent grandmother dominating the kitchen and ruling the household. Now she even misses her fussing and her nagging. Until now her world had always had grandmother sitting at its heart subtly directing the family and that is how it ought to be. How will they manage without grandmother as a sounding board and peacemaker?

Despite individual differences psychological theory recognises a common pattern in the 'healthy' grieving process. This is the emotional path taken as the individual faces the change in their world caused by the death, and then learns to adjust to living without that person. Bowlby (1980) identified the stages of mourning as:

Stage 1: Numbing: The first response to a sudden death may be apparent calm due to emotional shutdown. Initial feelings may be suppressed or the reality of death denied.

Stage 2: Yearning, searching, anger: The bereaved person starts yearning for the person who has died, expecting them every moment and hoping that they will reappear. Then they are likely to feel angry, particularly with anyone who can be held responsible for the loss. They may also get untypically angry about anything else that goes wrong in day to day living. Feeling angry with the deceased for leaving them is also quite common.

Stage 3: Disorganisation and despair: The world is a place of confusion and turmoil. The death is now accepted but there is the loss of security and stability. With that may come feelings of depression or hopelessness, anxiety or loneliness and perhaps guilt and self-reproach. The bereaved individual may have difficulty working and carrying out everyday responsibilities because they feel distracted, unmotivated, and unable to concentrate or tired.

Stage 4: Reorganisation: The bereaved person begins to adjust to the new reality, to the world without the person who has died. Although they can still miss and be sad, they begin to cope with everyday life. They may take over roles formerly carried out by the deceased.

With *adjustment* the bereaved person can start to make new relationships and invest in the future.

However the bereaved individual does not move smoothly from one stage to the next; they may move back and forth between stages, perhaps having a brighter moment of reorganisation and then plunge back into despair and depression. Wells (1988) suggests that for children the initial stages of intense grief may be shorter but that each new experience of loss brings back the feelings of intense sadness. With teenagers feelings may be 'bottled up' and turned inwards on themselves. If they do not have the opportunity to talk through their feelings, the grief may be expressed as odd behaviour and clinical depression. Then they require professional help.

Needing professional or psychiatric help

An adolescent may be acutely depressed and unable to function in everyday life or may turn to drugs or alcohol or have suicidal thoughts (see earlier chapters). Murray-Parkes and Weiss (1983) have described the circumstances which may lead to this pathological grief:

- A sudden death.
- The death of someone young.
- Multiple bereavements piling up.

- The individual's own psychological make-up.
- A social situation which does not encourage mourning.
- Social isolation and lack of support.

Wells (1988) suggests that teenagers also need professional help if they show signs of the following:

- Uncontrolled behaviour.
- Intense vulnerability, even to small separations.
- Complete absence of **any** show of feelings.
- Anorexia.
- Severe insomnia.
- Hallucinations.

Wells also quotes a psychiatrist:

> *Adolescents take life more seriously than they are given credit for, and their depression is often anger turned inwards. If this is not recognised, it may turn to blind rage, as they feel increasingly abandoned.*

> Wells, 1988: p16.

A supporter also needs to take talk of suicide seriously as some adolescents do commit suicide after a death of someone close to them. The reasons can be any of the following:

- A wish to be reunited with the dead person.
- Wanting revenge against the dead person.
- Wanting to destroy themselves to assuage guilt.
- Feeling that life without the person is not worth living.

For ways of responding to suicidal talk – see Chapter 14.

The adolescent's GP should be a first point of referral. If the young person is unwilling to consult a GP, then the youth worker should immediately seek advice from their supervisor about other referral points and how to proceed.

Other loss

This chapter has focused on loss caused by death of a significant person because that is the ultimate loss creating the greatest need for support. However an adolescent may suffer other distressing loss such as the death of a pet animal, a close friend emigrating overseas, a parent leaving home due to parental separation or divorce, or an older sibling leaving home. Others may perceive a particular loss as being relatively trivial, but the adolescent suffering the pain of separation may still have to pass through the stages of grieving. Again the young

---

Case study: Darren

17 year old Darren was serving an apprenticeship as an electrician. On day release at a local college he got into a serious fight with another student. This was reported back to his employer.

The employer, Jim, called him in to explain his erratic behaviour. Darren was a fast learner and seemed brighter than previous apprentices but his behaviour let him down. Sometimes he was the worse for drink and at other times he could get angry over nothing or just depressed. Jim, a family man with grown up children, was a patient listener and built up a relationship with Darren as they worked together.

From a particular outburst when Darren accused Jim of being 'just like his father', he began to ask about Darren's family. Darren had moved far from home and into lodgings to get away from his father. It took some weeks for the family story to come out. The once happy family had been shattered when Darren was 12 years old. Walking his six year old brother home from school, the younger boy ran suddenly into the road to avoid a dog and was hit by a car. He died within 24 hours. Darren had not gone to the funeral. His family never discussed the accident...At 14 he had started to drink heavily. At 16 he had left home to get away...but he still could not escape...

Darren was persuaded to get professional help...but the process was slow...

Twelve year old Darren had needed care, support and space to talk. Instead the extended family and friends were concerned with his parents and he was ignored. His parents were bound up in their own grief and he felt sure that they blamed him. He may have benefited from some professional help earlier. Five years on talking to a counsellor helped him to make some emotional sense of what had happened so that he could eventually allow himself to move on.

---

person may need the opportunity to talk and the time to adjust. It helps to have someone who will listen, acknowledge the loss, try to understand and show that they care.

Further reading

Kubler-Ross, E. (1969) *On Death and Dying*. London: Tavistock Publications.
Murray-Parkes, C. (1996) *Bereavement: Studies of Grief in Adult Life*. London: Routledge.

Chapter 16

Leaving Home

This chapter focuses on the emotional support required by a young person in the process of leaving home. Ideally the leaving should be planned but often the decision to leave is sudden or forced. Ways of exploring the decision to leave are suggested; the qualities that a young person needs to thrive independently are given. The leaving process can be slow and a young person may experience set-backs on the route to independence. It is helpful to have a trusted adult who can provide some permanence and be someone to turn to when things go wrong.

Leaving home is a significant milestone in the transition to adulthood. Ideally, before leaving, the adolescent should be well-prepared both materially and emotionally because living independently can be more difficult than it first appears. The adolescent who moves out of the family home but has a good relationship with their parents or guardian can be secure in the knowledge that there is still someone to turn to if things go wrong.

Unfortunately, for some adolescents, leaving home can be an abrupt and unsupported experience with unhappy consequences. Some young people decide that leaving home is the only option because they are victims of violence or abuse or because living at home is becoming increasingly uncomfortable. This may be because they are maturing or because the family dynamic is changing, or both. Many believe that having independence will be a liberating experience, only to find that the responsibilities of everyday living are more onerous than they had imagined. Some just do not manage and they end up homeless. When anticipating leaving home or having just left, an adolescent may seek outside help.

An explosive row with one or both parents is frequently a trigger for moving out. A parent, no longer able to control their adolescent and fearful of the effect of bad or deviant behaviour on their other children, may force the issue by offering an ultimatum: 'You obey the rules or leave!' The youngster who no longer recognises the need for parental authority will be only too pleased to take up the challenge for the prize of independence. A naïve adolescent may arrive with bag in hand at the local housing office or youth advisory centre, expecting immediate accommodation because they are homeless, only to find that their situation does not entitle them to immediate housing.

Case study: Just before Christmas...

Sadie, aged 16, arrived at the welfare desk five days before Christmas. On the previous evening she had been 'thrown out' by her mother and she had spent the night on a friend's floor. However, the friend's parents had made it clear that she could not stay over Christmas and now she had nowhere to go. She asked for an address of a hostel while she got herself sorted out.

The welfare officer, fearful that this vulnerable young woman would end up on the streets, could have reacted by immediately looking for a hostel. However she took her into a small side area where they could sit uninterrupted. She needed to know more about Sadie before acting. As the story unfolded it became clear that the mother-daughter relationship was under strain, aggravated by the mother having a new live-in partner and the expectations of Christmas. The previous night's row was nasty and her mother's opinions of her had been 'unforgivable'...but their relationship had once been good.

Although Sadie's initial attitude to the welfare officer had been bolshy and demanding, the officer's calm non-judgmental attitude and genuine interest in Sadie's difficulties broke down some barriers and rapport was established. Sadie was eventually able to listen to the options. None was ideal. Perhaps returning home was the lesser evil but how could she go back now?

The process was slow. The welfare officer left Sadie with coffee and a biscuit, while she saw to other clients. On her return Sadie decided that she could speak to her mother on the phone without disclosing her position. She was surprised by her mother's positive reaction and she agreed to phone again later that day. Some six hours after her first appearance at the office, Sadie was going to see her mother...but just to talk...and she would be back to get the address of the hostel. She did not return to the office.

Not all problems can be so speedily resolved. Many young people leave home after a row and travel away from their hometown, often to a big city where they cannot be found. They become 'missing persons', never making contact with their families and often sleeping rough or falling into the hands of people who exploit them.

Exploring the decision to leave home

Confronted by a distressed adolescent who has just left home and needs help to find accommodation for that night, the inexperienced youth worker can feel panicked into immediate action. 'If I don't get hold of social services before they close, he'll have to come home with me!' However, this is the moment to remain calm, to keep boundaries and to practise counselling skills (see Chapters 2 and 3). Find an appropriate place to talk because the reasons for leaving home *now* need to be explored:

- Ask gently why 'now' is the time chosen to leave home.
- Listen carefully. If the story is related at length, don't interrupt until they have finished. They need to be able to hear their own story and digest it.
- If little is said then do prompt gently for more information:
  - *With whom have you been living?*
  - *What happened today?*
  - *Do your parents or guardians know that you have left?*
  - *Has something changed at home recently?*
  - *Has there been anything in your behaviour which may have upset your parents or guardians?*
- Check their age – options vary for those over 18, for 16 and 17 year olds and for the under 16s.
- Check whether there has been abuse or violence in the home? If so, and the young person is under 18, then the social services may offer accommodation if the young person would be in danger and thus cannot return home. All social services departments provide an 'out of hours' service. If you cannot find the phone number, the police will be able to provide it. If you cannot contact your local social services or your supervisor, obtain advice from one of the organisations listed at the end of this chapter. Make sure that you consult the social services department (see Chapter 2 on child protection issues).
- If the young person is not in danger explore what would need to happen for them to return home? Is one parent likely to be amenable to discussion? Would a 'cooling off period' make a difference? Is there a relative or friend who would accommodate them for a night or two?
- If appropriate explore the benefits of leaving home and the disadvantages, such as:
  - The need for money to pay for rent, food and bills.
  - Have to do own shopping, cooking, washing and cleaning.
  - Loneliness. If move away – loss of friends and local network.
  - If unwell, no-one to care for you.
- Explain the dangers of moving to big cities.
- Money and housing are both major considerations. Although by law the local authority will assess homeless and vulnerable people, young people who have left home voluntarily do not necessarily qualify for accommodation. While 16 and 17 year olds can get benefits, again they may not qualify.
- If you are not an expert in housing laws, where the rules and guidelines quite frequently change, refer the young person to the local authority housing department or advice centre, so that they can find out the difficulties they are facing first-hand.
- Arrange for the young person to come back to see you when they have found out whether they can get accommodation and claim benefits.
- **A young person may initially state that they need to leave home, but this may be the symptom of other problems.** If these problems can be addressed then they may no longer feel the need to leave home.

- If a young person is to survive independently they need to be able to find their own way around the systems. If they understand the difficulties they are facing they may decide that this is not a good time to leave home. If they are ready and prepared to leave home then they will be able to undertake the practical arrangement for themselves.
- Meanwhile, accommodation is needed for tonight. If going home remains out of the question, explore other family members or friends who may provide a sofa or a floor. **Do not take the young person home with you**. Consult the contacts at the end of the chapter.

Planning how to leave home

An older adolescent facing an increasingly untenable situation at home or antici-pating a crisis may tell a trusted adult that they are planning to move out. The process of leaving home has been studied particularly in relation to preparatory work with young people living in foster families or 'looked after' by the local authority. Aldgate, Maluccio and Reeves (1989) pointed out that young people cannot just leave care at the age of 18 and know how to flourish independently. They need support both on the practical side (somewhere to live, a job or income and money skills) but also with the emotional side. They need to learn how to establish and maintain relationships and also to be able to deal with loss and grief. Leaving home in itself is a situation of loss.

While some years ago no proper provision was made for 'looked after' young people once they reached the age of 18, now most local authorities in the UK do have policies for helping the young people to leave care (Broad, 1998). Broad suggests that to leave home successfully an adolescent requires:

- somewhere to live
- financial support
- the desire to leave home
- a resilient personality
- a network of supportive friendships
- homemaking skills

Ideally they should also have:

- educational qualifications
- good employment and earning potential
- good health
- an agreed time to leave home
- a mature personality
- supportive parents or home-base

Adolescents leaving home and needing support are unlikely to have all the qual-ities on the first list, let alone the ideal extras. The supportive adult or youth worker can only hope to address some of the areas themselves and refer other matters on to experts. However by discussing all the different practical matters that need to be organised, and by sorting out priorities and time estimates, a young person can be helped to see that they are progressing towards independence. Over time, capabilities in the different areas can be monitored until they feel ready and a time for leaving can be set. Anyone who takes on the role of being a supportive adult and providing some permanence should remain available, within boundaries, for future advice and support.

Ideally leaving home is a gradual process. Kenny (1987) likened it to the *strange situation* in Attachment Theory whereby a small child can cope with a strange new environment if their adult attachment figure (usually their mother) is nearby. The toddler has the confidence to leave their mother's side or the small child goes just beyond the garden gate to venture into the big wide world and then hurries back to their *secure base*. Similarly leaving home for an adolescent is much easier if the home, or at least the people in it, remain as a secure base to which they may return. During this period of transition an adolescent still needs a 'caring' adult who will provide some permanence and stability. In a planned and supported leaving a parent or other adult will provide advice and remain a resource as, for example, somewhere for borrowing money, leaving belongings and contacting in an emergency. Young people sometimes leave home for a little while and then return.

Case study: To-ing and Fro-ing

17 year old Raj was alone when his mother died suddenly. As he had no other family in the UK he felt bereft but was made welcome by the family of his closest school-friend, Tom. Raj felt fairly comfortable with Tom and his family while they were both at school, studying for A levels, but he began to worry about what would happen when Tom went away on a planned gap year before university.

While Tom passed his A-levels with flying colours, Raj, affected by his grief, did poorly. When Tom went off travelling, Raj felt that he had to move out and become independent. He had some money from the sale of his family's home and he decided to rent a room, take a part-time job and retake his A levels. However after six weeks he had lost his job and could no longer bear living in his small room alone. He found himself back on Tom's parents' doorstep and they took him in again. This pattern repeated itself several times with Raj managing to live independently for longer periods at a time, but needing to return to Tom's home for periods of respite. It took four years for Raj to settle into a job and get permanent accommodation. Only then was he able to take up a place at university.

For all sorts of reasons it may take time for an adolescent to get used to living away from home. Students going away to university have the opportunity to make the transition gradually, perhaps spending term-time in college accommodation with respite periods at home for the vacation. Vulnerable young people who have to fend for themselves will also benefit from the chance to return home for a short time, to be looked after again, and to rebuild their internal resources before returning to live independently.

When things go wrong

Even the best-planned moves can go wrong. Provision cannot be made for all eventualities such as the loss of a job (vital for paying rent and bills), the breakdown of a relationship (with flat mates or with girlfriend or boyfriend), accidents or ill-health. A major change in situation, or even a minor one, may require a complete 're-think' of the situation and perhaps even moving back home again. This may be a great disappointment and a loss: it is undoubtedly difficult to have to re-adjust to parental house rules and inquisitions after a period of independence. However an outside adult or friend may be able to rescue the young person from feelings of failure and inadequacy. As with other loss (see Chapter 15) it may be helpful to talk over the circumstances and the distress it has caused. Caution against taking hasty decisions, allowing time for consideration and readjustment. Once readjusted the young person may be ready to start planning again, now with the benefit of experience. Sometimes the young person will need another boost of support to branch out for the second time, especially if their family have expressed their lack of confidence in the young person's ability to become independent.

Reconnection and reconciliation

Sometimes, after a few months away, adolescents regret leaving home. They realise that they have made a serious mistake but, perhaps they can see no way back to resuming a relationship with their parents. Any reconnection or attempts at reconciliation need to be handled sensitively and cautiously. Much pain has already been caused and amateur bungling by an outsider may make matters worse! Matters to be taken into consideration include the following:

- The parent may be reluctant to have the adolescent back home: life may have become much easier without them.
- The young person's behaviour may have been less acceptable than they have admitted to you.
- The young person may have developed further problems (e.g. drugs, illness, pregnancy) with which the parent may be unable to cope.
- If the young person loses their temporary accommodation by moving back home and that breaks down again, they may then be truly homeless.
- Despite loneliness and hardship, the young person might actually have a better chance of succeeding by living away from their parents, even if contact is resumed.

Occasionally a good family friend may be called on to act as mediator but, generally, it is best to refer matters to a professional counsellor, mediator or family therapist, who can help parents and adolescent to re-establish a connection. Together they may gradually work out a way forward which will be best for the young person.

Providing valuable support

However, do not underestimate the role that you can fulfil by just being a figure of permanence and providing emotional support. You can demonstrate that the adolescent is an individual whom you value and whom you believe will manage to live independently and successfully. An ongoing trusting relationship with you may provide the confidence to ask other adults for help. Listen to the problems and the grumbles. Be sympathetic and patient. Your resilience in a rocky relationship will show that relationships can have 'ups and downs' but still survive. Your acceptance of mistakes and apologies and of ongoing respect can be a helpful model for handling future relationships, including friendships. A young person may be able to live independently just because they know that you are there for emergencies, even if they never call on you.

Contacts

Helpful website: http://www.youthinformation.com (From menu – Leaving home)

First Key
Help for those responsible for providing services for young people in and leaving care.
0113 244 3898
0113 243 2541
http://www.first-key.co.uk/

Get connected
A free helpline for young people who are vulnerable or homeless – will put them in touch with various services. Service available 5pm–11.30 pm.
020 8260 7373
0800 096 0096
admin@getconnected.org.uk

Message Home Service
Free helpline – operating 24 hours per day. Operator will pass messages. Service is confidential and the caller details will remain private.
020 8392 4550
0800 700 740
http://www.missingpersons.org

National Society for the Prevention of Cruelty to Children (NSPCC)
020 7825 2500
0808 800 5000
http://www.nspcc.org.uk/

Shelter
Provides advice, information and support to people with housing problems or homelessness throughout Britain. Telephone service – 24 hours a day.
020 7505 2000
0808 800 4444
http://www.shelter.org.uk/

SECTION FOUR: REFERRING AND ENDING

Chapter 17

Referrals and Endings

The ending of a helpful relationship may be even more significant than its beginning. A bad ending or a mishandled referral may feel like a rejection. This chapter suggests ways of preparing and dealing with different endings: referrals to specialists or agencies, planned endings and unexpected endings.

The way in which a relationship ends is important. This is particularly so with vulnerable or troubled adolescents who have suffered repeated experiences of disappointment and rejection in their lives. An abrupt ending may be perceived as yet another rejection and all the earlier benefits of the relationship may be abandoned, wrecked or 'rubbished.' In best practice the ending needs to be kept in mind from the beginning so that the adolescent is prepared. This may be more easily said than done but any preparation for the end of a relationship is better than none and more helpful than an uncertain drifting away.

Most people find endings difficult and often avoid them. We may say 'See you later' instead of 'Good-bye' because we do not want to experience the feelings of loss that go with endings. However it is the responsibility of the youth worker or mentor to finish their good work properly by making the ending as positive as possible while acknowledging that some sadness is inevitable.

Ending just a short encounter

Even a single encounter is improved by a good ending. If you have met a young person and given encouragement and support then they will feel valued and respected if you have allowed time for a non-hurried ending.

In Chapter 4 there was a suggestion that, near the start of the meeting, the youth worker should mention how long they can spend together. This indicates that time is limited and helps the young person to anticipate the ending. The youth worker is responsible for the timing. It is also helpful to mention the time either ten minutes or five minutes before the end. Alerting the client enables them move on to the important things they want to say – rather than feeling short-changed when you run out of time.

Time near the end can be used to sum up what has been discussed and to go over any information or advice that has been given. It may be important to check how the young person is feeling and to consider what is to be done next. You may offer to meet again. If that is not appropriate then you may acknowledge that although you cannot help directly in this matter, you can still be approached again on other matters.

Referrals

When recognising that a young person's difficulties fall outside your area of expertise, you need to consider how to deliver that information without causing alarm or a feeling of rejection. If you listen to a problem and then respond too quickly that you can't help but someone else can, the youngster may misinterpret your lack of confidence and get the impression that their problem is really serious and that, perhaps, they cannot be helped or are not worthy of help. They may also feel very let down if they invested a great deal of emotion in daring to confide the problem to you – only to feel dropped like a hot potato – or to worry that their darkest secret is about to be shared by many strangers. In such situations the young person may not have the confidence or willingness to go to speak to a stranger, particularly an adult in a formal setting, such as a clinic, hospital or office.

The art is to create a good enough relationship first, so that the young person can trust you. They need the time and space to get used to talking about the problem with you listening. You need time to hear and consider why referral might be the best option and how to present that. They will then be more likely to accept your considered judgement about the need for referral and to think about any persons or agencies that you recommend. Your role as a 'stepping-stone' to further help is vital but it is considerably more than just supplying an address or telephone number on a piece of paper. It is the positive experience of your relationship which will encourage them to dare to embark on another relationship, perhaps with a professional who initially appears to be unapproachable.

Reluctance to take up referral

Some of the reasons for not taking up a referral may involve feelings of:

- Shame of having to disclose the difficulties again to a stranger.
- Fear of what may happen.
- Lethargy for self-protection. By doing nothing the problems may go away or be coped with best alone.
- Lack of confidence.

There are no easy formulae to combat these obstacles but a patient and understanding approach can help.

The fact that the young person has admitted the problem to you, or let you find out, indicates that at some level they want help. Disclosing for the first time may have been a lengthy process involving considerable anxiety and stress. However having 'told' once, the next telling may not be so hard. They now have a way of talking about the problem and you can discuss how they can explain it to someone else. You may be able to assist the referral by sending a brief note or letter or making a phone call or making an appointment where appropriate. Discuss with the young person what is to be written or said and obtain their permission to do so, so that they remain in control, so reducing some of the anxiety.

Fear about what may happen next may be realistic. It should not be minimised if referral may involve big changes. It is best countered by explaining the next stages and the reasons for them (see below). The more you know about how colleagues or specialists in different fields operate, the better you will be able to inform the young person and so prepare them.

Lethargy and doing nothing are the most difficult to counter. By not acting the young person can pretend to themselves that there is no problem or that they are able to handle it alone, perhaps by self-discipline. Where time is on your side you can repeat the options of referral each time you meet and discuss why action is better than leaving things as they are. You can express your own concerns for their well-being and, where appropriate, explain that you can still give support. Where time is critical (pregnancy, health concerns, suicidal thoughts, criminal offending) you may need to be more pushy and forthright about the consequences of doing nothing. Whatever the circumstances it is helpful to consult your supervisor or colleagues.

Preparation

Preparation can alleviate some of the anxiety and reluctance. A young person needs to be forewarned about intake procedures and waiting lists because they can be very off-putting. If they know about a six-month waiting list before their first clinic appointment, they will not have raised expectations of immediate help. Initial questioning can also be daunting. The more the young person knows about what to expect, the more comfortable and less threatened or persecuted they may feel in the strange situation. For example, questions about parents, living conditions or ethnicity may appear very intrusive and discriminatory. It is helpful to explain that some questions are asked to directly help the individual while others, such as monitoring of ethnic background, may be to ensure that an agency is being used by the whole population and is not being discriminatory. Medical referrals can be frightening too. For example, if a young pregnant teenager understands the reasons for and the procedure involved in an internal examination, then she will cope better with the experience.

Lack of confidence in approaching formal organisations or embarrassment about filling in forms also causes anxiety. Sometimes talking about the people they will meet at an agency and if possible giving some names will give a young person the courage to venture over the threshold. For example: 'Sue is the person at the receptionist desk. She's friendly and will spend time taking down your details. There will be forms to fill in but she can help with those. You just have to ask her.' 'Dr Hussain is a young female psychologist.' This sort of information will give an impersonal organisation some human faces. The young person may agree to you to phoning ahead so that Sue will be expecting them. Overall, good preparation will support the referral and promote its success.

Ongoing or informal support

When a relationship continues after a referral, it is necessary to pay attention to and maintain boundaries. A youth worker may keep seeing the adolescent in daily life, meeting in the youth centre or for ongoing work such as educational mentoring or youth offender schemes. It is natural and caring to ask whether the young person has taken up the referral but the skill is not to break the boundaries of that relationship.

The new relationship with, for example, the counsellor or the doctor to whom you have referred, is not your business. However interested or concerned you may be, you must not interfere with that relationship or what happens within it. The young person may find it difficult to make a new relationship and come to say that they would prefer to be talking to you. Remain supportive of the new professional. The course of therapy or treatment about to be started may call for a major change or a challenging commitment. It would be easier to escape them and come back to you. Alternatively the new counsellor may be portrayed as a threatening or persecutory tyrant. Remain detached and have confidence in the professionalism of the person or agency that you recommended.

The young person who feels comfortable talking to you may also want to discuss what has taken place in therapeutic sessions. However interesting or flattering, do not be drawn in. The essence of the counselling or therapy may be in confronting the difficulties with the therapist. If you start working on those difficulties outside the sessions you may be diluting or even undoing their good work. Similarly, if there are decisions to be made or options to be chosen, that too may be part of the therapy. You can remain supportive but detached by explaining to the young person that you cannot get involved because this is not your area of expertise. That is why you suggested the therapist, doctor, agency etc. Do not get involved in the action, but do encourage the adolescent to keep attending appointments and co-operating.

Sometimes the informal ongoing role of the youth worker may be to keep the young person functioning within the community or to help them to reintegrate with an appropriate peer group as treatment progresses (see Chapter 10 for examples). This can be done without getting involved in the therapeutic relationship or the work within it.

There is also a fine balance to be maintained in allowing the adolescent to become independent of you. Unless explicitly asked to do so, your role is not to monitor behaviour. Learning to live as an adult in the community might involve making some mistakes or having some slips. Try to remain supportive and non-judgmental. The therapist has responsibility for the treatment; they will respond to minor slips or major lapses.

Your responsibility is to maintain your relationship within its boundaries. However, you may eventually consider that you have contributed all that you can for a particular individual who now has good alternative support. There may be other calls on your time by young people with urgent needs who have no other support. This might be the time to plan an ending.

Planned endings

Most supportive relationships eventually come to an end. The problems about which you were consulted may have been resolved. Other reasons for ending include the young person growing out of the age-group for whom you mainly cater, losing interest in your main activities, moving away or problems increasing such that residential treatment is required. Alternatively you may be on a fixed contract which is ending, or moving away or getting a new job or gaining promotion which lessens the availability of one-to-one contact. Whatever the reason it is the responsibility of the youth worker to anticipate the ending as far ahead as possible.

Again preparation is the key to retaining positive valuing of the relationship. If it is the youth leader who is leaving, the young person may still feel abandoned and angry at being left but they will have a chance to get used to the idea. The youth leader should set out a timetable so that the young person will be aware of the date of a final meeting. Even if diaries or calendars have not featured previously, this is a good time to introduce them:

- Plan how many meetings you can fit in before the final one.
- If meetings have been weekly, it may be appropriate to reduce their frequency to once a fortnight, etc. The young person will grow more independent.
- Use the last few meetings to review what has happened and to recognise how much they have changed since you first met or the different skills they now have. Take stock of their current abilities.
- Discuss what their next steps should be and whether they will need further help.
- If immediate referral or handing on is not necessary, discuss how they can get help and from whom, should they need to do so later.
- Discuss how the last meeting will be. Acknowledge sadness and loss on both sides. Express what you have valued in the relationship. This will give them the chance to think about the ending.
- Do not promise to keep in touch, unless you are one of the very few who really will keep up regular correspondence or a routine of phone calls. Most people cannot and it is better to be honest about this than to promise and disappoint.
- Set a final meeting date.
- If referral is to take place, sort it out well before the last meeting.
- At the final meeting give yourselves time to talk about the good and the bad times: to celebrate achievements and to acknowledge sadness at the ending.
- Finding that they can cope maturely with the ending will be a valuable experience in itself. Endings like death can be mourned but then the survivor moves on.

Unplanned endings

Unfortunately endings are not always so neat and tidy. Some cannot be anticipated. A young person may be moved away without warning by family or by
those looking after him. Sometimes a crisis in your personal life such as illness or
difficult home circumstances means that you have to end one or more relationships
abruptly. It is not always possible or appropriate to explain the reasons to the
young person, but if it is at all possible a final meeting should be arranged so that
the youth worker and adolescent can at least have a face-to-face ending. If you are
in turmoil, do consult your supervisor who can remind you of the different issues
to be considered and give you support.

During that final meeting you need to address the following:

- The young person is not the cause of this relationship coming to an end.
- You value the relationship and do not want the good parts to diminish just
  because you are no longer meeting.
- The external cause for the ending was not anticipated. The lack of preparation
  may result in uncomfortable or painful feelings of loss for both.
- The young person should be allowed to express anger, disappointment,
  sadness, etc. Do not fight it. Just express your sorrow.
- If there is someone to take over, discuss what they would like you to pass on.
- Express own sadness and regret but point out the positive changes achieved
  so far or that the relationship itself has been important.
- Again, do not make promises about keeping in touch that you cannot keep.
- Explain that although you will say good-bye, you will remember the rela-
  tionship because of its positives.

If a final meeting is not possible, then a letter or phone call might serve as an
ending.

Adolescent groups moving on

In many youth groups the individual is part of a small internal group of friends
and when most of the group outgrow the organisation the individuals tend to
leave at much the same time. It is not always an openly discussed leaving and
may be more of a drifting away. It may coincide with the start up of a new interest
or with the onset of school exams or with leaving school. Where a group is
leaving or has left, the youth leader can suggest a party, event or celebration to
mark the leaving. Such an event is significant for those who are leaving and those
left behind. It shows that the leaving members made a contribution and were
appreciated by those following them; it also signals to those left behind that the
group with its remaining members and leaders is of value and worthy of a formal
leave-taking. Again the mixture of celebration and sadness of leaving can be a
useful experience. It also gives the youth leader the opportunity to acknowledge
that adolescents are expected to develop and mature and that the leaving of

childhood or early adolescent pursuits is healthy and to be welcomed. Endings can be good.

During the stages of leaving there may be the opportunity for the youth leader to acknowledge and celebrate the achievements of the shy or troubled individual. Just a private moment at the edge of the party scene can be a valuable moment for the young individual to feel special and be recognised for their contribution to the group and the achievements of their personal development. Take time to remember an incident requiring personal courage, a time when temptation was resisted, a brave apology or the slow conquering of a difficulty. Such personal acknowledgement may stand the individual in good stead for the future. It is from past experiences that we take our values and lead our lives.

Further reading

Leigh, A. (1998) *Referral and Termination Issues for Counsellors.* London: Sage.

Chapter 18

A Final Word

The theme throughout this book has been the value of developing a good, trusting relationship with an adolescent. This is the core ingredient for responding to and helping a young person. The basic counselling skills needed to engage in such a relationship have been described, as have those steps required to bring the relationship to a satisfactory end. The importance of maintaining boundaries and considering child protection and other ethical issues has also been stressed, as responsible working practice ensures the safety of both youth worker and young person. The book has also indicated the obligation for youth workers and mentors to think about the context of their own lives, their culture and their prejudices, before working with young people. Only then will they be prepared to genuinely try to understand other young people, each with their particular parental and peer relationships embedded in a specific culture or mixture of cultures. The backgrounds to a selection of different problem areas have been outlined with guidelines for approaching some common difficulties but neither the range of problems nor the problem areas can cover the vast range of difficulties that youth workers and mentors will meet in practice.

Every individual adolescent brings new challenges and new opportunities for understanding from the youth worker or mentor. The very shy, intimidated or withdrawn young person may take a great deal of patient trust-building before a relationship can even start to develop. Just encouraging such a person to talk a little or to meet at all may need a lot of skill and dedication. Another young person may hide self-doubt and fear behind a mask of bravado, toughness and disdain for outside help. Again a patient and persevering approach with a calm and non-judgmental attitude may eventually find a chink in the defences and a way to engage. Initially youth workers can bring availability, consistency and reliability to the young person. Only once there is real engagement can the youth worker and client work together to explore present difficulties. Although different chapters in the book looked at different areas of problems, in real life, individuals tend to have an enmeshment of several difficulties and no two individuals are quite the same. Differences in personalities and circumstances will mean that ways of working with each will be unique.

But the youth worker or mentor may not be able to help. This book has highlighted many problem areas which require specialist or professional support. In these circumstances providing the route to that specialist help and giving support until the contact is made is in itself very valuable. In other cases the way forward may not be at all clear. However, the youth worker should not be working alone and consulting with supervisors, managers or colleagues may help to redefine the problems and suggest different options for discussion with the young person. Sometimes a young person's situation is really difficult and the prospects bleak. Serious illness or death in a family, parental strife or imprisonment may have to be faced. If the youth worker or mentor can just remain available, open and genuinely supportive then that sense of company through the bad times may help a little. Sometimes even that is not possible.

The importance of supervision was stressed in Chapter 2 and has to be reiterated. Working with young people, particularly those in need of support can be exhausting and mentally debilitating. After an adolescent has unloaded misery, despair or rage on to the youth worker, who has controlled their own body language, thought about their responses, absorbed some of the emotions and so contained the young person's anxiety, they may be ready to kick the furniture. Initially a colleague might be a convenient listener but a supervisor will allow time to explore the youth worker's concerns and feelings and to look at the problems from different perspectives. The supervisor will also monitor the emotional capacity of the youth worker or mentor, indicating when they are over-stretched and should at least reduce their caseload. This will be in the best interests of all their clients.

We all make mistakes. It is by making mistakes that we learn. And just as we explain to adolescents that life is about taking calculated risks, so it has to be in our own practice. However, if, in regular supervision, we are used to owning up to our mistakes and are ready to acknowledge that we can be wrong, then when an error of judgement or other mistake does occur we can receive support while we try to limit the damage and make amends. A supervisor will help to ensure that the young person still gets the best support available.

Working with adolescents can be both rewarding and frustrating. Some young people will be open to new ideas, willing to learn from their mistakes and able to take support when things are not going according to plan. Working with them will be rewarding. However, those who really need support are the individuals who can be the most frustrating because they vacillate between desperately needing immediate help at times of crisis and stubborn independence in the calm between the storms. They will be unreliable, poor at keeping appointments or keeping in touch and just when you think they are making progress or changing their behaviour in the right direction, they will backslide or roam off course again. However, if you and they can bear the frustrations, then together you may be able to forge a relationship which will help to make a few beneficial and sustained changes in their lives. These may be small but nevertheless rewarding.

This book is only an introduction and it can be no substitute for experience and training. However it has been written with the hope that it will provide inspiration for readers to develop their own abilities to support young people. Truly helping just one young person can enrich the life of the helper too.

References

Adams, G. R. and Gullotta, T. (1983) *Adolescent Life Experiences*. Monterey, CA: Brooks/Cole.

Aldgate, J., Maluccio, A. and Reeves, C. (1989) *Adolescents in Foster Families*. London: B.T. Batsford.

Allen, I., and Dowling, S. B. (1998) *Teenage Mothers: Decisions and Outcomes*. London: Policy Studies Institute.

Allison, K., Leone, P. E. and Spero, E. R. (1990) Drug and Alcohol Use Among Adolescents. In Leone, P. E. (Ed.) *Understanding Troubled and Troubling Youth*. Newbury Park, CA: Sage.

Banks, S. (Ed.) (1999) *Ethical Issues in Youth Work*. London: Routledge.

Barber, J. S. and Mobley, M. (1999) Counselling Gay Adolescents. In Horne, A. M. and Kiselica, M. S. (Eds.) *Handbook of Counselling Boys and Adolescent Males*. Thousand Oaks, CA: Sage.

Bor, R., Miller, R. and Goldman, E. (1992) *Theory and Practice of HIV Counselling: A Systemic Approach*. London: Cassell.

Bowlby, J. (1980) *Attachment and Loss, Vol. 3: Sadness and Depression*. London: Hogarth Press; New York: Basic Books.

Broad, B. (1998) *Young People Leaving Care: Life after the Children Act 1989*. London: Jessica Kingsley.

Brooks-Gunn, J. et al. (1986) Physical Similarity of and Disclosure of Menarcheal Status to Friends: Effects of Age and Pubertal Status. *Journal of Early Adolescence*. 6: 3–14.

Brown, B. B., Mory, M. S. and Kinney, D. (1994) Casing Adolescent Crowds in a Relational Perspective: Caricature, Channel, and Context. In Montemayor, R., Adams, G. R. and Gullotta, T. P. (Eds.) *Personal Relationships During Adolescence*. Thousand Oaks, CA: Sage.

Burnard, P. (1989) *Counselling Skills for Health Professionals*. London: Chapman and Hall.

Caldwell, C. (1999) Counselling Depressed Boys. In Horne, A. M. and Kiselica, M. S. (Eds.) *Handbook of Counselling Boys and Adolescent Males*. Thousand Oaks, CA: Sage.

Cass, V. (1996) Sexual Orientation Identity Formation: A Western Phenomenon. In Cabaj, R. and Stein, T. (Eds.) *Textbook of Homosexuality and Mental Health*. Washington DC: American Psychiatric Press.

Coleman, J. C. and Hendry, L. B. (1999) *The Nature of Adolescence*. 3rd edn. London: Routledge.

Cragg, A. et al. (1993) Safer Sex and Sexual Health: Understanding Young People. In Glanz, A. McVey, D. and Glass, R. (Eds.) *Talking About It*. London: Health Education Authority.

Darling, N., Hamilton, S. F. and Niego, S. (1994) Adolescents' Relations With Adults Outside the Family. In Montemayor, R. Adams, G. R. and Gullotta, T. P. (Eds.) *Personal Relationships During Adolescence*. Thousand Oaks, CA: Sage.

DoH (2002) *Fertility: Conceptions, England* www.doh.gov.uk/HPSSS/TBLA13.

Dishion, T. J. (1990) The Peer Context of Troublesome Child and Adolescent Behaviour. In Leone, P. E. (Ed.) *Understanding Troubled and Troubling Youth*. Newbury Park, CA: Sage.

Dockrell, J. et al. (1993) Sex, HIV and AIDS: Behaviours and Beliefs of Sexually Active Young People – Heterosexuals, Gay Men and Male Sex Workers. In Glanz, A. McVey, D. and Glass, R. (Eds.) *Talking About It*. London: Health Education Authority.

Donnellan, C. (Ed.) (1997) *The Abortion Debate: Issues for the Nineties (Vol. 34)*. Cambridge: Independence.

Donnellan, C. (Ed.) (1998) *Coping with Eating Disorders (Vol. 24)*. Cambridge: Independence.

Donnellan, C. (Ed.) (2000) *Self-harm and Suicide (Vol. 51)*. Cambridge: Independence.

Dowling, E. and Gorell Barnes, G. (2000) *Working with Children and Parents through Separation and Divorce*. Basingstoke: Macmillan.

Eating Disorders Association. (1998) Anorexia Nervosa. In Donnellan, C. (Ed.) *Coping with Eating Disorders*. Cambridge: Independence.

Eating Disorders Association. (1998) Bulimia Nervosa. In Donnellan, C. (Ed.) *Coping with Eating Disorders*. Cambridge: Independence.

Egan, G. (1990) *The Skilled Helper: A Systematic Approach to Effective Helping*. 4th edn. Pacific Grove, CA: Brooks/Cole.

Furman, W. and Wehner, E. A. (1994) Romantic Views: Toward a Theory of Adolescent Romantic Relationships. In Montemayor, R. Adams, G. R. and Gullotta, T. P. (Eds.) *Personal Relationships During Adolescence*. Thousand Oaks, CA: Sage.

Gaine, C. (1995) *Still No Problem Here*. Stoke-on Trent: Trentham Books.

Geldard, K. and Geldard, D. (1999) *Counselling Adolescents*. London: Sage.

Gibb, S. (1997) Going on to a Boom or About to go Bust, Does Mentoring Have a Future? In Stephenson, J. (Ed.) *Mentoring: The New Panacea?* Dereham: Peter Francis.

Graham, J. and Bowling, B. (1995) *Young People and Crime*. London: Home Office.

Haughton, E. (1995) *Dealing With Stress*. Hove: Wayland.

Hill, P. (1993) Recent Advances in Selected Aspects of Adolescent Development. *Journal of Child Psychology and Psychiatry*. 34: 69–99.

Holman, B. (1981) *Kids at the Door*. Oxford: Blackwell.

Holman, B. (2000) *Kids at the Door Revisited*. Lyme Regis: Russell House Publishing.

Hudson, F. and Ineichen, B. (1991) *Taking it Lying Down: Sexuality and Teenage Motherhood*. Basingstoke: Macmillan.

Imam, U. F. (1999) Youth Workers as Mediators and Interpreters: Ethical Issues in Work with Black Young People. In Banks, S. (Ed.) *Ethical Issues in Youth Work*. London: Routledge.

Irwin, J. (2002) *Still No Idea* www.getconnected.org.uk/info/publications/still no idea.doc.

Jaffe, M. (1998) *Adolescence*. New York: John Wiley.

Jaffee, S. R., Caspi, A. and Moffitt, T. E. (2001) Predicting Early Fatherhood and Whether Young Fathers Live with their Children: Prospective Findings and Policy Reconsiderations. *Journal of Child Psychology and Psychiatry*. 42: 803–15.

Kaufman, S. (2001) Detached Youth Work. In Factor, F. Chauhan, V. and Pitts, J. (Eds.) *The RHP Companion to Working with Young People*. Lyme Regis: Russell House Publishing.

Kenny, M. E. (1987) The Extent and Function of Parental Attachment Among First-Year College Students. *Journal of Youth and Adolescence*. 16: 17–29.

Kenny, M. E. (1994) Quality and Correlates of Parental Attachment Among Late Adolescents. *Journal of Counselling and Development*. 72: 399–403.

Kent, V. and Davis, M. (1993) Social Interaction Routines in Heterosexual Encounters of Young People. In Glanz, A. McVey, D. and Glass, R. (Eds.) *Talking About It*. London: Health Education Authority.

Kiselica, M. S. (1990) Counselling Teen Fathers. In Horne, A. M. and Kiselica, M. S. (Eds.) *Handbook of Counselling Boys and Adolescent Males*. Thousand Oaks, CA: Sage.

Kubler-Ross, E. (1969) *On Death and Dying*. London: Tavistock publications.

Leigh, A. (1998) *Referral and Termination Issues for Counsellors*. London: Sage.

Leonard, S., Lee, C. and Kiselica, M. S. (1999) Counselling African American Male Youth. In Horne, A. M. and Kiselica, M. S. (Eds.) *Handbook of Counselling Boys and Adolescent Males*. Thousand Oaks, CA: Sage.

Leone, P. E., Walter, M. B. and Wolford, B. I. (1990) Towards Integrated Responses to Troubling Behaviour. In Leone, P. E. (Ed.) *Understanding Troubled and Troubling Youth*. Newbury Park, CA: Sage.

Luxmoore, N. (2000) *Listening to Young People in School, Youth Work and Counselling*. London: Jessica Kingsley.

Mabey, J. and Sorensen, B. (1995) *Counselling for Young People*. Buckingham: Open University Press.

Macdonald, D. I. (1984) Drugs, Drinking and Adolescence. *American Journal of Diseases of Children*. 138: 117–25.

Marchant, H. (1989) Supervision: A Training Perspective. In Marken M. and Payne, M. (Eds.) *Enabling and Ensuring Supervision in Practice*. Leicester: National Youth Bureau.

Maychell, K., Pathak, S. and Cato, V. (1996) *Providing for Young People: Local Authority Youth Services in the 1990s*. Slough: NFER.

McKay, A. (1989) Non-managerial Supervision. In Marken, M. and Payne, M. (Eds.) *Enabling and Ensuring Supervision in Practice*. Leicester: National Youth Bureau.

Moore, S. and Rosenthal, D. (1993) *Sexuality in Adolescence*. London: Routledge.

Moore, S., Rosenthal, D. and Mitchell, A. (1996) *Youth, AIDS and Sexually Transmitted Diseases*. London: Routledge.

Morgan, S., and Banks, S. (1999) The Youth Worker as Confidante. In Banks, S. (Ed.) *Ethical Issues in Youth Work*. London: Routledge.

Muisener, P. P. (1994) *Understanding and Treating Adolescent Substance Abuse*. Thousand Oaks, CA: Sage.

Murray-Parkes, C. (1993) Bereavement as a Psychosocial Transition: Processes of Adaptation to Change. In Dickenson, and D. Johnson, M. (Eds.) *Death, Dying and Bereavement*. London: The Open University and Sage.

Murray-Parkes, C. and Weiss, R. J. (1983) *Recovery from Bereavement*. New York: Basic Books.

National Mentoring Network (2002) http://www.nmn.org.uk/ [26.12.02]

Nelson-Jones, R. (1997) *Practical Counselling and Helping Skills: Text and Exercises for the Lifeskills Counselling Model*. London: Cassell.

Newman, D. A., Horne, A. M. and Webster, C. B. (1999) Bullies and Victims. In Horne, A. M. and Kiselica, M. S. (Eds.) *Handbook of Counseling Boys and Adolescent Males*. Thousand Oaks, CA: Sage.

Noller, P. (1994) Relationships with Parents in Adolescence: Process and Outcome. In Montemayor, R. Adams, G. R. and Gullotta, T. P. (Eds.) *Personal Relationships During Adolescence*. Thousand Oaks, CA: Sage.

Noonan, E. (1983) *Counselling Young People*. London: Methuen.

Norton, R. (2001) Re-evaluating Refugees. *Young People Now*. 141: 26–7.

Norton, R. and Cohen, B. (2000) *Out of Exile: Developing Youth Work with Refugees*. Youth Work Press.

Olweus, D. (1994) Annotation: Bullying at School: Basic Facts and Effects of a School Based Intervention Programme. *Journal of Child Psychology and Psychiatry*. 35: 1171–90.

Owens, R. E. (1998) *Queer Kids: The Challenges and Promise for Lesbian, Gay and Bisexual Youth*. London: Harrington Park.

Page, R. C. (1999) Counselling Substance-Abusing Young Males. In Horne, A. M. and Kiselica, M. S. (Eds.) *Handbook of Counselling Boys and Adolescent Males*. Thousand Oaks, CA: Sage.

Pelzer, D. (1997) *The Lost Boy*. London: Orion.

Phoenix, A. (1991) *Young Mothers?* Oxford: Polity.

Porteous, D. (2001) Mentoring. In Factor, F. Chauhan, V. and Pitts, J. (Eds.) *The RHP Companion to Working with Young People*. Lyme Regis: Russell House Publishing.

Raphael, B. (1994) *The Anatomy of Bereavement*. Northvale, NJ: Jason Aronson Inc.

Raskin, P. M. and Waterman, A. S. (1994) On the Bidirectional Impact of Counselling on Identity and Intimacy Developments. In Archer, S. (Ed.) *Interventions for Adolescent Identity Development*. Thousand Oaks, CA: Sage.

Rice, K. G. and Mulkeen, P. (1995) Relationships with Parents and Peers: A Longitudinal Study of Adolescent Intimacy. *Journal of Adolescent Research*. 10: 338–57.

Robbins, P. R. (1998) *Adolescent Suicide*. Jefferson, NC: McFarland and Co.

Rodgers, B. and Pryor, J. (1998) *Divorce and Separation. The Outcomes for Children*. York: Joseph Rowntree Foundation.

Ross, P. (2002) *Despair and Suicidal Thinking* www.reading.ac.uk/Counselling/counselling/Desperate Despair and Suicidal Thinking.

Ross, P. (2002) *Self Help for Self Injury* www.reading.ac.uk/Counselling/counselling/Self Injury.

Royal College of Psychiatrists. (2000) Deliberate Self-harm in Young People. In Donnellan, C. (Ed.) *Self-harm and Suicide*. Cambridge, UK: Independence.

Rutter, M., Giller, H., and Hagell, A. (1998) *Antisocial Behaviour by Young People*. Cambridge: Cambridge University Press.

The Samaritans. (2000) Signs of Suicide Risk. In Donnellan, C. (Ed.) *Self-harm and Suicide*. Cambridge, UK: Independence.

The Samaritans. (2002) *Young People and Suicide* www.samaritans.org.uk/know/youngpeople.

Scott-Cameron, N. (2000) *Bad Hair Day? A Guide to Dealing With Everyday Stress*. Shaftesbury: Element.

Sharp, S. and Smith, P. K. (1991) Bullying in UK Schools: The DES Sheffield Bullying Project. *Early Child Development and Care*. 77: 47–55.

Sheffield University. (2002) *Confidentiality Issues for Staff* www.shef.ac.uk/drugs/manage/ confide.

Smith, M. (2003) The End of Youth Work? *Young People Now*. 5–11 Feb.: p1.

Stein, M. and Carey, K. (1986) *Leaving Care*. Oxford: Basil Blackwell.

Sue, D. W. (1981) *Counselling the Culturally Different: Theory and Practice*. New York: John Wiley and Sons.

Sue, D. (1999) Counselling Asian American Boys and Adolescent Males. In Horne, A. M. and Kiselica, M. S. (Eds.) *Handbook of Counselling Boys and Adolescent Males*. Thousand Oaks, CA: Sage.

Sue, D. W. et al. (1998) *Multicultural Counselling Competencies*. Thousand Oaks, CA: Sage.

Taylor, A. M. (1997) *Parental Attachment and Adjustment to College for Adolescent Students in Further Education*. Unpublished Ph.D. Thesis, Birkbeck College, University of London.

Thorne, B. (1990) Person-centred Therapy. In Dryden, W. (Ed.) *Individual Therapy*. Milton Keynes: Open University.

Weinstock, A. (2003) Connexions. *zero2Nineteen*. Feb. p11.

Wells, R. (1988) *Helping Children Cope with Grief*. London: Sheldon.

Wheal, A. (1998) *Adolescence: Positive Approaches for Working with Young People*. Lyme Regis: Russell House Publishing.

Wright, M. (1997) Depression in Childhood and Adolescence. In Varma, V. (Ed.) *Troubles of Children and Adolescents*. London: Jessica Kingsley.

Young, K. (1999) *The Art of Youth Work*. Lyme Regis: Russell House Publishing.

Youniss, J. A., McLellan, J. A. and Strouse, D. (1994) 'We're Popular, but We're Not Snobs': Adolescents Describe Their Crowds. In Montemayor, R. Adams, G. R. and Gullotta, T. P. (Eds.) *Personal Relationships During Adolescence*. Thousand Oaks, CA: Sage.

Youth Justice Board. (2002) *Youth Survey 2002* www.youth-justice-board.gov.uk.